Marketing concepts for libraries and information services

Marketing concepts for libraries and information services

SECOND EDITION

Eileen Elliott de Sáez

facet publishing

© Eileen Elliott de Sáez 1993, 2002

Published by
Facet Publishing
7 Ridgmount Street
London WC1E 7AE

Facet Publishing (formerly Library Association Publishing) is wholly owned by
CILIP: the Chartered Institute of Library and Information Professionals.

Eileen Elliott de Sáez has asserted her right under the Copyright Designs and
Patents Act 1988 to be identified as author of this work.

First published 1993
Second edition 2002
Reprinted 2003

British Library Cataloguing in Publication Data
A catalogue record for this book is available from the British Library.

ISBN 1-85604-426-2

Typeset in 11/15pt Aldine 401 BT and Syntax by Facet Publishing.
Printed and made in Great Britain by MPG Books Ltd, Bodmin, Cornwall.

CONTENTS

Dedication

To Juan

ACKNOWLEDGEMENTS

In the first edition of this book I said that I should like to acknowledge the influence that so many writers and practitioners in the worlds of marketing and librarianship and information have had on the writing of this book. I repeat that here, and would like also to pay tribute again to the work of Professor Philip Kotler, who persuaded me, along with very many others, that marketing is a people business, that it can be applied in all fields, and that it can be fun.

Any book depends on the support and encouragement of others in its production. The second edition is no different from the first in that my thanks are due again to all the editors at Facet Publishing for their expertise and patience. I am appreciative of the reception of the first edition too. My husband, Juan, and my family were as always unfailing in their encouragement and my gratitude to them is deep felt.

INTRODUCTION

The digital world is changing the functions of libraries and information services, and the role of the librarian and information professional is as vital as ever in developing the knowledge and skills of the individuals in the communities they support. Cyberm@rketing, e-commerce, e-mail marketing, relationship marketing, data mining, wired marketing: this is marketing in the digital age. It is about narrowcasting as much as broadcasting, or mass marketing, but *'the right service to the right person at the right time'* in the digital world of marketing has a very familiar ring to librarians and information professionals.

Marketing concepts and techniques can contribute a dynamic approach to total strategy development for librarians and information professionals that will ensure effective management, the achievement of goals and the creation of a confident blueprint for the future. The real value of marketing is to ensure the survival and growth of the libraries and information services, which exist to enhance the communities they serve, adding value to the lives of the people and organizations who are their users, customers and clients.

The marketing model in the digital age focuses on users, clients and customers and on keeping them. Managing user and customer relationships in the context of sweeping change, delivering the marketing mix appropriate to user groups, creating a product and service delivery of quality that is recognized, appreciated and rewarded are key issues. They always were, they always will be. What is clear from past experience is that libraries and information services, and librarians and information professionals, have an enormous capacity to change and adapt. The themes discussed here are intended to generate strategic marketing thinking that will aid that evolutionary process.

Libraries and information services are, more than ever, multifunction organizations with multiple goals in a so-called information world where information is power and a potent, and sometime expensive, commodity. An information world where the individual who has access and skills in information seeking can be in the curious dilemma of being advantaged thereby and at the same time suffer the stress of information excess and overload. At the same time those denied such access, without the skills, can exist in a world of famine, both virtual and real.

Visions of the future of the information world are still as imprecise as they are exciting: librarians, information scientists, information managers, information consultants, records managers, information officers, information brokers, database managers, documentalists, knowledge managers, web information managers and data miners already operate in the electronic environment of information supermarkets, gateways, portals, systems, telecommunications networking and global change. Throughout this text, 'libraries, information services and information centres' and 'librarians and information professionals' are used to encompass the multifaceted nature of professionals and services in the current information world.

The absolute key to successful strategic change, if libraries and information services are to prosper, is to focus on the user. Information consultants have no illusions on this score: a client who is not satisfied will go elsewhere. Professionals in libraries and information services must put user commitment first on their list of priorities. The 'user' includes the regular user, the irregular user, the non-user and the potential user. Who is the user? What are the influences on the user? What does the user value? How might we better inform and educate the user? These are not questions that should daunt the librarian or information professional who is proud to be in the people business. Nor should the new techniques of data mining or customer-centric business intelligence, discussed in this book, hold any fears for the professionals who are well able to transfer their information skills to exploit the data available.

Librarians and information professionals do have an affinity with marketing philosophy, concepts and practice despite their sometimes reluctance to embrace marketing. A recent study showed many academic library directors 'were uncomfortable with the public relations aspect of their job' (Marshall, 2001, 119). A report commissioned by the British Library Research and Development Department (Aslib, 1992, 19) concluded that in libraries 'there was a lack of knowledge and skills in marketing and related disciplines, although there was a thirst for knowledge about them'. Ten years on, and although the situation is changing, marketing is still too often equated to promotion only. In the public sector too many libraries are closing needlessly and in the commercial sector there is a dangerous trend to rely on intranet, extranet and internet, leaving the management of these to the information technologists rather than information professionals. In the preface to the millennium edition of *Marketing management*, Philip Kotler says: 'This new world is also characterised by an amazingly rich information environment . . . the World Wide Web and e-commerce are dramatically altering the marketing landscape' (2000, xxvi–xxvii). Kotler's 'infomediaries' (2000, 670), however, are not information professionals, but websites operating online shopping services.

There are good examples in the library world where marketing is producing success: Bucharest libraries operated an open-air library in Bucharest University Square during June 2001 as part of a hugely successful marketing effort, The Rediscovery of Reading, aiming to energize a community in the process of regeneration.

The aim of this book is to ensure that librarians and information professionals understand marketing concepts and can apply marketing techniques. The chapters on customer relationship marketing and e-marketing reflect the concerns of today's marketers and are rooted in those concepts and techniques. Senior managers in libraries and information services who are responsible for framing their organization's corporate mission and strategic plan will look to their colleagues and staff to assist them in planning processes, as well as in implementation, of marketing strategy. Internal marketing is therefore as important as external marketing.

This book is addressed primarily to practising librarians and information professionals in senior and middle management; students of information and library management may benefit from it too. It is presented in the strong belief that marketing will make the difference that will ensure the survival, growth and development of library and information services.

References and further reading

Aslib (1992) *Sponsorship in libraries*, vol. 1, Report and survey.

Kotler, P. (2000) *Marketing management: the millennium edition*, 10th edn, Prentice Hall.

Lovelock, C. and Wright, L. (1999) *Principles of service marketing and management*, Prentice Hall.

Marshall, N. J. (2001) Public relations in academic libraries: a descriptive analysis, *Journal of Academic Librarianship*, **27** (2), 116–21.

O'Connor, J. and Galvin, E. (2001) *Marketing in the digital age*, 2nd edn, Financial Times/Prentice Hall.

1

WHAT IS MARKETING?

Marketing is the management process which identifies, anticipates and supplies customer requirements efficiently and profitably.

(The Chartered Institute of Marketing)

The objectives of this chapter are:

- to define marketing
- to discuss why librarians and information professionals need to understand marketing concepts
- to identify what can be marketed, including librarians and information professionals themselves.

Librarians and information professionals are in the people business; they now need to operate as business directors and managers and must harness marketing concepts and techniques to their other very considerable powers if their services are to survive, offer quality and prosper.

The newcomer to marketing concepts realizes very quickly that marketing abounds wonderfully in common sense and that concepts that are put into practice work. Marketing is about:

- collecting information
- forecasting trends
- consulting all concerned

- understanding markets
- formulating objectives
- planning strategy
- implementing strategies
- evaluating everything
- communicating with everybody.

Publicity and promotion do not appear in the list, deliberately. Publicity and promotion are an important part of marketing, but only part, and can be effective only if the marketing foundations are sound. Attempting to publicize that which the business no longer needs, promoting services when access to them is severely restricted, offering stock or specialist advice to users who are indifferent or unable to take advantage, not only wastes precious resources but destroys the credibility of the professionals behind the promotional activities. Glossy brochures and bannered web pages cannot disguise a failing service.

Marketing and management

Marketing is a management discipline, and equally it is part of organizational and management philosophy, reflected in attitudes and approaches across the whole organization. Marketing provides the focus for successful organizations. The starting point lies in recognizing that 'marketing deals with identifying and meeting human and social needs' (Kotler, 2000, 2). Librarians and information professionals, well used to providing for both, should be heading for success.

Knowledge, resources, planning, all have their place in strategic marketing development and will be put to most effective use where marketing strategies are underpinned by a whole organization approach. Effective strategy development will encompass cultural, political and cognitive facets as well as financial considerations.

Marketing needs to be practised effectively within the organization as well as without and library and information managers need to recognize that within

includes within their own service and also the interaction of their personnel with the wider organization.

The culture of an organization, be that organization a pan-global company,
a library or an information service, will derive from the shared assumptions,
beliefs and vision of the members of the organization. These beliefs include
a perception of the organization in which they are working, for example
whether it is dynamic, always at the forefront, or whether it is old-fashioned,
slow to change; it might be environmentally conscious or politically immured.
Members accept the organization's operational styles and, essentially, its rituals – rituals that often cloak a powerful structure of influence. The
understanding of the political nature of the organization and its power bases
at the cognitive level will enhance the information professional's ability to
manage strategic change and develop a marketing ethos that can be collec-
tively owned.

Marketing, the librarian and the information professional

Managers have traditionally devoted most of their time to the management
of money, materials, machines and men, information coming a very poor last,
if at all, as Kotler said in 1984 (187). Information in the 21st century is now
recognized as a commodity to be valued in all spheres. Are we then looking
at a world in which the librarian and information professional can at last truly
play an influential part? What is the role of the librarian in a free society? How
powerful and influential could the person be who has control of society's
knowledge (Elliott de Sáez, 1993, 3)? In all spheres, information professionals
and librarians can be key players. But it will be their ability to market themselves that will make the difference.

Librarians and information professionals will need to recognize that developing effective marketing strategies is more difficult today, not because of the
digital revolution, but because of a society in which customers are becoming more sophisticated and knowledgeable, maybe even cynical, about
marketing activities (Coulter, 2002, 174). In the new macro-marketing environment, where the world is literally at the marketer's fingertips, the library

or information service must 'create the market by combining a good grasp of customer needs with creativity and technological know-how' (Lambin, 2000, 40). Marketing intelligence, the information flows, digests and analyses of the library or information service markets, will only convert to competitive intelligence when the organization listens to its users and also analyses what they are *not* saying. To compete effectively for the time, energy and support of users, readers and clients, all library and information services must identify what their competition is and why it is succeeding in the same market.

Much has changed in the marketing of libraries and of information services in the time since Cronin introduced his selection of classic papers on marketing. 'The value of intelligent marketing cannot be overestimated, particularly in relation to non-monopolistic service organizations such as libraries,' he said (1981, 2). The papers still repay study today; classics such as Levitt's 'Marketing myopia' (1960) and Kotler's 'Strategies for introducing marketing into nonprofit organizations' (1979) are referred to in every major marketing text.

In 1991, a major study of how marketing was implemented in the public libraries of the USA (Kinnell and MacDougall, 1991) found no clear pattern emerging as to how marketing was managed; marketing planning was still in a process of development. The survey revealed a general lack of awareness and understanding of the full implications of marketing strategy and much confusion over terminology at most levels in local authorities.

In the 21st century, a much greater awareness of the value of marketing is abroad, there has been an expansion in the professional literature, and libraries are beginning to employ designated marketing officers who are dually qualified as information professionals and marketing professionals. But while branch libraries are closing, big companies are outsourcing their information needs, and school libraries are giving way to computing departments in the fight for resources, there is still a very long way to go.

Marketing and the quality revolution

Where substantial progress has been made, in libraries and information services across all sectors, is in the quality revolution. The father of the quality dimension in management, W. Edwards Deming, identified the role of the customer as a priority: 'customers must get what they want, when they want it, and how they want it' (Neave, 1990, 32). Johnson (1999, 137) says that there has been 'an uncompromising emphasis on the need to satisfy customers' wants and expectations'. Johnson also quotes Ray Wild: 'In the search for productivity the correct starting point is the marketing concept. Productivity is not an end in itself but one of the means to an end; and that end is consumer satisfaction' (1999, 137). Wild (1995) on the management of quality and the marketing function should be obligatory reading for library and information service managers reviewing their quality approach and mechanisms. It is a model of clear and practical exposition of the most important quality mechanisms balanced with a philosophical viewpoint, and his text is customer oriented throughout.

The essence of quality delivery in the marketing of services is now crystallized in SERVQUAL, a quantitative technique for measuring service quality (Palmer, 1998, 161). SERVQUAL derives directly from the research of Parasuraman, Zeithmal and Berry (1985), which identified the following as essential factors of service provider and customer concern:

- access
- reliability
- credibility
- security
- customer expectations
- responsiveness
- courtesy
- competence
- communication
- tangible evidence.

SERVQUAL is discussed in Chapter 8 under 'Market research techniques'.

Marketing services

> Productivity and people are the keys to the future . . . probably more labour-intensive services will emerge to satisfy new needs as the demand for skills and knowledge to cope with the new environment or leisure requirements increases. . . . Service marketing needs to be considerably developed over the next decade.
>
> (Cannon, 1992, 227)

Prophetic or simply a good marketer analysing the market?

Librarians and information professionals can be relieved that it is not the case that the marketing of services differs considerably from the marketing of products. The same basic principles apply and in many sectors it is often difficult to disaggregate the service and product offering.

The service sector, of course, does have special characteristics, usually identified as:

- intangibility
- inseparability
- variability
- perishability.

Thankfully, this does not mean that our fellow professionals are wraiths and die young. *Intangibility* refers to the fact that services cannot be touched or seen or tasted, unlike physical products. Nevertheless, who can calculate the effect of a smile at the right time, a soothing voice in a crisis? How many patients have benefited, unknowingly, from the skill not just of the surgeon, but the librarian behind him or her?

The chocolate bar once consumed has gone forever. A service is offered and experienced or consumed at the same time, the processes are *inseparable*.

The *variability* of the quality of the service offered can be very considerable as a result of the factors that constrain the service. Services do vary: staff ability, motivation, training and personality cannot be controlled in the same way as the weight of chocolate bars.

Services cannot be stocked or warehoused and are deemed therefore *perishable*. Perishable in the sense that they cannot continue to be offered, as for example when an aircraft seat is available on a particular journey on one date at a particular time. However, this type of perishability is not a problem for librarians and information professionals who would be better advised to think in terms of product offering or proposition in relation to their services.

The differences between product and service marketing are well argued by Jobber (2001, 684), who says that the service provider can demonstrate 'tangible clues' to performance, illustrating happy holiday makers in holiday company brochures or checklists following the servicing of a car. The information unit needs to produce physical reports on its activities and performance, the benefits it offers clients. Libraries need to put physical evidence of their presence everywhere in their communities: opening times on posters or bookmarks in every 'waiting area' locally, whether rail or bus station, medical clinics or student cafeteria, would make a good start.

What can be marketed?

Anything can be marketed: products, services, organizations, people, places, social issues. Products can range from apples to zoos, services from plumbing to psychotherapy, or people from presidents to pop singers. Libraries, information centres, learning resource centres, information services, librarians, information professionals, learning resources managers, information managers – all can be marketed successfully too.

Products and services

The core business of the library and information service is the range of products and services that provide benefits for users and that answer users' most important needs, whether for commercial intelligence, or education, leisure, recreation or social needs. That core business is information.

The design of information products, how information might be customized, packaged and delivered, is now a concern for all librarians and information professionals, whereas once it would have been an issue only for those in the commercial sectors. The design of the information product defined by Yerbury et al. (1991, 129–37) is a 'planned solution to an information-handling problem . . . based on knowledge of the user, knowledge of the subject matter and knowledge of how to present the message'. A thoroughly sound marketing approach.

Any and all of the services offered by the library or information service can be marketed successfully: lending services, interlibrary loans, online searching facilities, housebound readers' services, increasingly, access via licence to other services. Information consultants and information service companies exist in a variety of contexts and there is enormous, often unrealized, potential in public and academic libraries for staff to offer consultancy services too. The literature on consultancy in the academic sector is drawn together by Frank et al. (2001, 95), who say that 'librarians must aggressively customize, filter, synthesize and market information for students, scholars and administrators'. The role of the librarian as information consultant in this context includes working with researchers to obtain funds and to package research information appropriately, to track trends and to work with academics, students and research scholars to facilitate progress. In the public and private sectors, librarians and information professionals could undertake contract work on specific projects. These projects could be for local businesses, authorities or organizations in the case of public librarians and for information professionals in the commercial sector; the clients might also be national or local government or organizations in a non-competitive area. These services would need to be marketed as over and above the 'norm' of information services and priced accordingly.

There are some products that are obvious because of their affinity to the products we all recognize in a consumer-based society – publications, badges, plastic bags, calendars, collections of photographs, local maps, bookmarks and mugs are among the products seen on sale in most public and most academic libraries.

Then there are the cafeteria services, the walks to haunted places, the storytelling sessions, the information technology tuition, the local history lectures, the rare treasures exhibitions – all to be marketed.

Organizations

The library or information unit can be marketed as an entity itself, as an organization. Examples of successfully marketed organizations are many and wide ranging: in the commercial area British Airways, for example, in the charitable the World Wildlife Fund, in the cultural the Louvre, and even in the military the Royal Air Force. Governments, political parties, religious movements and professional bodies provide further excellent examples.

Organizations do not 'exist in a world separate from our understanding of them. We must actively interpret and make sense of them. . . . Some writers on management have suggested that organizations should be thought of as theatres or psychic prisons which dictate the ways people think and act' (Wickham, 2000, 191–2). Corporate image management is founded on the 'marketing premise that everything an organization does, and does not do, affects the perception of that organization and its performance, products and services (Howard, 1998, 2). Libraries and information services will have to conform to the corporate image of their parent organization but they must not hide within it.

Corporate identity and corporate image are discussed in Chapter 9.

People

Presidents and prime ministers, pop stars, personalities from the world of sport and entertainment, all provide daily proof of good marketing strategy being practised. How often does the library and information world practise this very effective method of reaching the required targets? The appointment of a new branch manager to a bank or building society reaches every edition of local newspapers and who remembers whether he or she has two children, a red setter and a penchant for harp music? The message retained is of new blood, something stirring, so why do library and information personnel, on the whole, dislike the idea of communicating in this way with their potential markets? Every new member of staff should be asked to support the service through announcements of their appointment. Every member of staff, including the senior librarians and information managers, must be encouraged to share news of interest with the media.

The personality cult today encourages the use of product and service endorsement and honour conferment. Cities across the world abound with streets and buildings named after dignitaries or men and women of renown, and a growing number of libraries, particularly in the academic sector, are using this method of honour conferment to show appreciation of services rendered to the community, or perhaps to the library itself. In the fast-changing fortunes of the business and political world it pays to take care in selecting such individuals and, as with similar sponsorship-type partnerships, it is advisable to consider decisions of this kind very carefully. It was not until 2001 that Liverpool Airport became John Lennon Airport, its motto 'Above us only sky'. It is very much a two-way process: the status and public perception of the person thus honoured enhances the service now bearing the new name. Librarians do have a status value in a community, whether that community is a small school or the national arena, and a plethora of such naming opportunities and consequent marketing potential can be found.

Where many academic libraries are operating self-service systems, the physical appearance of a librarian adds value to the service, albeit in the current terminology of the electronic converged academic services it will probably be a hybrid librarian. Why, particularly in the university sector, did such a dreadful descriptor appear? Would a marketing culture have allowed the escape of such a creature?

Places

Countries and counties, cemeteries and cathedrals are marketed with ease. Why not make a feature of the physical siting of the library? The British Library's new building has generated genuine and continuing interest among sectors of the public previously unaware of its existence. Any interesting facts about the library can be talked about in local or national media, tourist guides, in paper or web information sources of all kinds.

Place is discussed further in Chapter 4, but the following points are worthy of immediate consideration. The approaches to a library that is part of a larger organization or institution must be investigated. Are there decent signposts? Is the library on all the maps of the authority's or institution's geographical locations? Is the entrance attractive, but even more important is it obvious that the building or set of rooms is the library? Well-designed noticeboards and lettering are worth every penny, as they give an immediate impression of an organization that knows what it is about and is proud of its existence.

The small information unit in commercial premises, or perhaps the school library housed temporarily in spare classrooms, might be tempted to feel that this advice is not applicable to them. But while it is probable that information officers will have to conform to the company's corporate design policy, it will always be worthwhile to seek desirable change that will still be in keeping with the whole: a glass door rather than plain wood, or even no door at all, will succeed in a boring corridor of blank door after door. The school librarian might enlist the aid of the art teachers and the children themselves in creating an entrance worthy of a Father Christmas Grotto or a spaceship from *Star Wars*. The children's library which is part of the children's literature research foundation Fundación Germán Sánchez Ruipérez in Salamanca, Spain, was designed as a tree: storytelling and picture books in the roots (i.e. the basement) lead up to the leafy branches and tree of knowledge for older children (on higher floors). The teenage library was another creative area, the lower decks of a naval ship this time, bulwarks, hammocks and all.

Major structural alterations are not being suggested, but the use of imagination is. Why should libraries be called libraries? Unemployment centres have thrived as job shops, doctors' practices have become health centres, local authority swimming baths have become leisure pools, shopping centres are retail parks, some libraries have become learning centres, others are resource centres. In the UK, Newcastle upon Tyne's mobile library service to schools was welcomed happily as the Book Bus during the lifetime of the pension-age double decker that chugged around the city disguised as a bumble bee (buzz!), the Salamanca library is known as The Foundation. The Book Stop, Resource Shop, Kwik Loan, Information Works, the potential list is enormous. However Maurice's Doc. Centre simply does not have the romantic appeal of Harry's Bar, nor is it appropriate in a situation where the British Library Document Supply Centre commands a worldwide request-answering rate of four-million plus per annum (LISU, 2001).

There is still a real sense of place attached to 'the Library' and it is with relief that one notes that organizations as august as the World Bank and the International Monetary Fund advertised their complex automated network of speciality collections, the Library, and the chief executive, the Chief Librarian.

Social issues

Campaigns against alcohol abuse, smoking and the use of animals in testing, together with campaigns for healthier eating habits, sporting lifestyles and the reduction of energy consumption, number among the social issues marketed efficiently in recent years.

Libraries have played their part – in literacy schemes for adults, teenagers and babies, and in open- and distance-learning programmes, now becoming learning for life institutions. They have provided exhibition space for background information to support government public enquiries into local issues and even became a social issue themselves in the UK Library Campaign. The New Opportunities Fund in the UK supports a huge network of public-library-based information technology skilling activities through the Community Access to Lifelong Learning programme. A substantial government investment is aimed at the development of the necessary technical infrastructure: 'by the end of 2002 we expect all 3500 public library service points in England to have an ICT learning centre, and all will be eligible to gain the UK Online branding . . . it will serve as a badge of quality', said Alan Howarth, UK Libraries Minister, in May 2001.

Where do members of the community discover that this tremendous resource is available to them? The professional press has plenty of detail, there is little mention elsewhere. Moreover, why do public librarians have to wait for information and communications technology policies before recognition of their worth and a quality branding that leaves out the word, and concept, 'library'? There is real potential here for librarians and information professionals who believe in their role of enablers in terms of the knowledge of society to use their marketing skills to ensure that they are recognized as activists and not merely the passive receptors of technology.

Finally, marketing is a strategic level activity: it needs senior management involvement at all levels and it must be on all agendas. Librarians and information professionals must encourage and develop a marketing culture in their libraries and information centres and be prepared to market their own very considerable talents, experience and skills. Marketing needs resources, human as well as financial, and it needs teamwork. It cannot be done alone, even where the library or information centre employs, or has access to, a designated marketing manager. Marketing is a formula for success. The investment needs to be serious, and the rewards are immense.

References and further reading

Brown, S. (2001) Marketing for Muggles: Harry Potter and the retro revolution, *Journal of Marketing Management*, **17** (5–6), 463–79.

Cannon, T. (1992) *Basic marketing*, 3rd edn, Cassell.

Chapman, D. and Cowdell, T. (1998) *New public sector marketing*, Financial Times Management.

Coulter, M. (2002) *Strategic management in action*, 2nd edn, Prentice Hall.

Cronin, B. (ed.) (1981) *The marketing of library and information services*, Aslib.

Elliott de Sáez, E. (1993) *Marketing concepts for libraries and information services*, Library Association Publishing.

Frank, D. G. et al. (2001) Information consulting: the key to success in academic libraries, *Journal of Academic Librarianship*, **27** (2), 90–6.

Frieden, J. et al. (1998) Information as a product: not goods, not services, *Marketing Intelligence and Planning*, **3**, 1–13.

Howard, S. (1998) *Corporate image management*, Butterworth-Heinemann.

Howarth, A. (2001) Building the new age together, *Library Association Record*, **103** (5), 266.

Jobber, D. (2001) *Principles and practice of marketing*, 3rd edn, McGraw-Hill.

Johnson, B. (1999) *Introducing management*, Butterworth-Heinemann.

Kinnell, M. and MacDougall, J. (1991) Strategies for marketing public libraries and leisure services, *International Journal of Information and Library Research*, **3** (3), 167–85.

Kotler, P. (1979) Strategies for introducing marketing into nonprofit organizations, *Journal of Marketing*, **43**, (January), 37–44.

Kotler, P. (1984) *Marketing management*, 5th edn, Prentice Hall.

Kotler, P. (2000) *Marketing management: the millennium edition*, 10th edn, Prentice Hall.

Lambin, J.-J. (2000) *Market-driven management*, Macmillan Press.

Levitt, T. (1960) Marketing myopia, *Harvard Business Review*, **38** (4), 45–56.

LISU (2001) *Annual library statistics*, Library and Information Statistics Unit.

Lynch, J. L. (1998) *Corporate compassion: succeeding with care*, Cassell.

McKean, J. (1999) *Information masters: secrets of the customer race*, John Wiley.

McConnell, C. (2001) *Change activist*, Momentum.

Neave, H. R. (1990) *The Deming dimension*, SPC Press.

Palmer, A. (1998) *Principles of service marketing*, 2nd edn, McGraw-Hill.

Palmer, A. (2001) *Principles of service marketing*, 3rd edn, McGraw-Hill.

Parasuraman, A., Zeithaml, V. A. and Berry, L. L. (1985) A conceptual model of service quality and its implications for future research, *Journal of Marketing*, (Fall), 41–50.

Perry, R. (2001) *Marketing unwrapped*, John Wiley and Son.

Rowley, J. (2001) *Information marketing*, Ashgate Publishing.

Wickham, P. A. (2000) *Financial Times corporate strategy casebook*, Pearson Education.

Wild, R. (1995) *Production and operations management*, 5th edn, Cassell.

Yerbury, H. et al. (1991) Making the transparent visible: an activity to demonstrate some of the concepts of information service and product design, *Education for Information*, (June), 129–37.

2

THE CORPORATE MISSION

There are three kinds of organizations: those that make things happen; those that watch things happen; those that wonder what happened.

(Anonymous and quoted everywhere)

The objectives of this chapter are:

- to explore why the library or information service needs a mission statement
- to outline the elements of a good mission statement
- to discuss the relationship between corporate and marketing planning.

The corporate mission statement is a strong, clear declaration of an organization's beliefs about its own nature and distinctive competence. It must answer the following absolutely fundamental questions:

- What are we doing?
- Who are we doing it for?
- Why are we doing it?
- What should we be doing?

Not all libraries and information services will want to be the kind of organization that makes things happen; market leaders often spend resources and energy on being first, only to see the competition quietly and competently watch what happens, assess the situation, and come in with a better, more efficient and more effective product or service. But the library and information centre that has a clear mission, with well thought through, achievable objectives will never be in the third category of organizations in the opening quote.

The need for a mission statement

The mission statement embodies the aims and objectives of the library and information centre. A major marketing communication, it is a promotional tool internally as well as externally, since the listening and sharing that go into its making as all are consulted will promote the image of a caring organization. The involvement of personnel at all levels throughout the library or information service will provide a shared sense of direction, significance, opportunity and achievement.

Research shows that most successful company managers are those who attach importance to corporate values. Chisnall's (1989, 138–9) analysis concludes:

> . . . it is important to note, however, that professed commitment to high corporate values needs to be translated into practice: strong declarations themselves may sound impressive, but implementation has to be effected by management at every level of organisation and expressed in many ways, such as high standards of customer service, good teamwork between executives in different departments as well as in the same section.

The real encouragement to librarians and information professionals to put their users first in formulating their mission statement is that in Chisnall's findings those companies who ranked customer satisfaction as the most important corporate value were the companies that were highly profitable.

There are few organizations today that do not have some kind of mission statement. Too often they consist of a litany of promises, culled to sound good, from the latest management jargon and fads, and do not reflect the real ethos of the organization. As a result they fail to engage staff or convince customers and clients.

It takes time to prepare a good mission statement. It involves consultation at all levels and it requires an examination of past history, user needs and current and future resources. It must be forged with conviction and be capable of fulfilling expectations.

The mission should be clear on goals and objectives and provide a realistic foundation for strategic development. It is worse than useless to construct a taxonomy of resounding phrases. This fuels resentment at the apparent lack of recognition or understanding of the genuine need to specify commitments and purpose, and it wastes valuable resources and energy. Nor is it advisable to be too narrow in defining purpose: the provincial theatres that saw themselves as providers of dramatic representations, rather than being in the entertainment business, are closed. Levitt's 'Marketing myopia' (1960) gave the famous example of the railroad managers who thought they were in the railroad business rather than in the business of transport. The telephone company that sees itself as supplying customers' communication needs is more successful than the one that considers itself to be a supplier of telecommunication hardware. British Telecom's customer-care image initially brought it into admirable profitability; advertisements showed how their mobile phones rescued women on motorways, brought teenagers and parents together and became the bodyguards of the vulnerable. Multi-telephone homes have become the norm and we are now looking at 3G and blue tooth development in a growth of telecommunication for home users that has been exponential. With a massive information resource carried in the handbag or pocket, why should the general public or the business user need libraries?

Total-quality management and performance assessment are implicit in evolving the mission and marketing objectives for libraries and information services today. A vigorous enquiry into quality and marketing performance assessment conducted by Bonoma and Clark (1988) draws on the work of Steffire (1985) and Pirsig (1974) in their well-respected, first-class evaluation of assessment models. Steffire supports natural systems over goal-driven strategies in achieving marketing objectives and argues that the critical problem facing organizations is to remain adaptable and flexible enough to survive in a changing environment. Pirsig's work, *Zen and the art of motorcycle maintenance*, identifies the two types of personality that the mission statement would need to convince and empower. There are the people who are highly analytical and rational in their thought processes and who advocate logical argument, and the others, who would rather immerse themselves in the romantic, subjective side of reality, and leave aside arguments on cause and effects. Bonoma and Clark (1988, xiii) have a word of caution however: 'others have thrown themselves on the rocks of assessing marketing performance in the last fifty years with mixed, but always bloody, results'.

At corporate strategic and functional level, performance needs to be measured against objectives to manage the strategy effectively. The purpose and benefits of a total-quality management strategy are to focus the organization's potential to use resources effectively to achieve objectives. The British Library sees itself as a vital element in the national economy at the beginning of the 21st century. Its mission and marketing strategies will support that positive role. Hard Rock Café's credo 'Love all, serve all' sounds almost simplistic, but Tom Peters (1998, 473) says 'sounds like good business strategy to me. No, make that a "great" public/private/independent-sector strategy!'

A measure of the difficulty in deciding on an organization's mission and objectives and in producing the mission statement is the amount of unease and distrust encountered in introducing the task. It is a challenge to look at the library or information service and decide, objectively, what its real purpose is. The act of identifying a true focus for the future may throw previously accepted attitudes and practices into question, painfully. The involvement of staff at all levels, while seeking to identify the role of the library or information service, may well spotlight root causes of past or current conflict. Attitudes and perceptions are difficult to change: staff who have entered the organization at varying stages of the library or service development may have genuine cause to defend direction and priorities as seen from their standpoint of specialization, experience or conviction.

The staff of a public library might be at odds as to whether business, arts or community services should be highlighted. In an academic library, the encompassing of business or commercial services may fuel the debate on research conflicting with commercial interests; and the question of where priorities should lie between the needs of undergraduate students and those doing advanced research will produce equally heated arguments.

A number of libraries in the higher education sector are drawing back from their previous role of providing for the whole development of a student and are concentrating resources on supporting academic courses. Higher education institutions taking this stance defend their position on the grounds of dwindling resources, but they lay themselves open to the charge of providing cafeteria-style education.

An added dimension to the difficulties of constructing a mission statement for the library or information service is that, by its very nature, in the majority of cases the service will be part of a larger, complex organization. It will be essential to be in tune with the organization or authority mission, explicit or implicit.

Nevertheless, the library or information service needs to produce its own separate mission statement, since it can closely specify the particular priorities and objectives of the service, which will then provide the base for strategic planning and decision making. It can also set the agenda for the organization or authority performance assessment criteria for the library or information service.

Librarians and information professionals can learn from their colleagues in the profit-making sectors, taking the best ideas from their practices and honing them into effective tools. Barbara Walker, Confederation of British Industry, Associate Director for Marketing Policy (1993, 12) summed up comments at a series of marketing conferences for business directors:

> Companies are beginning to recognise and acknowledge the importance of human values – communication, involvement and empowerment.
>
> Chief executives or business directors . . . discussed customer services, and the need to talk to your customers, and your customers' customers; the need to talk to your suppliers and get their ideas for new products. They talked about knowing your market, benchmarking, team-building, the need to reward people for

success and not to punish too hard for failure. They talked about empowerment: in fact, about human issues, about the need for better communications and employee involvement. Research and technical directors . . . we asked them how they made their investment in innovation, in research and development work – and they were coming up with the same things: internal communications, getting the corporate strategy right, encouraging teamwork, encouraging people to take risks and not to stifle innovation and inventiveness.

Employee involvement and empowerment are vital in libraries and information services if they are to succeed in their mission and achieve their vision.

Vision and mission

'Vision' is beginning to replace 'mission' in the USA, whereas in Europe an organization will often have both a vision and a mission statement to work to. Where this happens, the mission statement tends to be very much the shorter-term objectives document, while the vision will be the executive view of the long term.

The American philosophy of producing a picture of the current situation and comparing this with the preferred vision of the future would seem to be more desirable, since there is no chance of confusing issues. Working towards the achievement of the vision becomes the corporate goal and because the vision is the ideal, a sense of purpose and energy is unlocked in the organization, leading thereby to greater self-fulfilment and satisfaction among organization members. There is no doubt, however, that the challenges presented by visioning can be sufficiently disturbing to cause organization tension. There may be attempts by some to obliterate the vision, because the pathway towards it is perceived as being fraught with difficulties, or because they see no place for themselves in the new picture or even because the vision initiator personally is disliked or feared.

Sample mission statements

The following are extracts from mission statements, or the closely allied Citizen's Charter approaches of organizations and libraries, which reflect the key issues.

From a multinational company:

- The strategic process for improving everything we do is to the benefit of our customers, ourselves, our shareholders and the community in which we operate.
- Continuous improvement of everything we do will take us towards the standard of the best imaginable.
- Everyone has customers. Delighting them is everybody's business.
- Every member of staff has an important contribution to make.

The Office of Arts and Libraries outlined 'The National Mission Statement for the Public Library Service' in *Setting objectives for public library services* (OAL, 1991, Chapter 5 'The mission statement'). It stated:

> The public library is a major community facility whose purpose is to enable and encourage individuals to gain unbiased access to books, information, knowledge and works of creative imagination and which will:
>
> - encourage their active participation in cultural, democratic and economic activities;
> - enable them to participate in educational development through formal or informal programmes;
> - assist them to make positive use of leisure time;
> - promote reading and literacy as basic skills necessary for active involvement in these activities;
> - encourage the use of information and an awareness of its value.
>
> The local and community nature of the service requires special emphasis to be placed on the needs and aspirations of the local community and on the provision

of services for particular groups within it, while also providing access to wider resources through regional and national library networks.

From a selection of UK public libraries, the following promises:

- the provision, without bias, of information on any subject
- priority to serving elderly people and those in need, who require special help to benefit from the service
- information on all subjects, as well as advice on how to use other sources
- to serve as the first point of enquiry about information on any subject which customers may need for research, leisure, business and an understanding of their rights
- information on matters of public interest readily available
- community information collections in every library
- library services for your whole community, paying particular attention to people with special needs
- will encourage children to read by arranging reading games and similar activities and by providing quality children's books in pleasant sur- roundings
- to hold material in designated major Indian languages and any other minority language for which substantial demand is evident
- books in languages other than English as appropriate to community needs.

From a large academic institution:

- to make a positive contribution to the development of a learning society and the economy
- to develop active partnerships with students, industry, the professions, busi- ness, commerce and the community, and so provide a distinctive profile of access and outreach
- to develop the capabilities, the enterprise and interpersonal skills of our students.

From a number of school libraries:

- to foster and develop equal opportunities for all races, genders and abilities
- to encourage competent, independent and critical learners by providing education for information handling and study skills
- to meet the curricular, cross-curricular, cultural and leisure needs of users by the selection of an appropriate range of resources
- to foster and develop critical reading, reading for pleasure and a research/information skills curriculum
- to ensure that users become effective information handlers and independent learners.

One of the most influential mission statements in the library world comes from the British Library. The British Library corporate plan, *Gateway to knowledge*, covered the years 1989–94 and the planning of the Library's move into new premises, certainly one of the most important events in its long history. Here was a clear statement that the purpose, or mission, of the British Library is to advance knowledge. Across the world and through the centuries, the British Library symbolized the conservation and advancement of knowledge, a corporate image to be admired and rarely emulated in the library world. There are, of course, many great libraries, but none has quite the majesty, or ability to trigger responses, as that of the British Library.

> The British Library, through its incomparable collections, is the world's leading national research library. . . . We celebrate and interpret our rich and varied collections to encourage the broadest possible awareness and accessibility of the nation's recorded heritage. (British Library, 1993, 9)

Corporate and marketing planning – the relationship

Characteristically a corporate plan will be fundamental in nature, concerned with the long-term and total organizational purpose. It will be the responsibility of directors and chief executives to formulate it. Marketing planning is an integral part of the overall plan. Research by Hooley, Lynch and Shepherd (1990) showed improved performance over competitors and a higher return on investment for companies who saw marketing as a guiding philosophy for the whole organization. Because of this, where the marketing function lies in the structure of an organization is a vital element in achieving success. The library or information centre may be one unit of a large and complex organization; it is imperative that it should have its own marketing champion.

Lambin (2000, 10) also reports that marketing is now more commonly a strategic-level activity:

the role of strategic marketing is therefore (a) to lead the firm towards existing opportunities or (b) to create attractive opportunities, that is opportunities which are adapted to its resources and know-how and which offer a potential for growth and profitability. The process of strategic marketing has a medium-to-long-term horizon; its task is to specify the firm's mission, define objectives, elaborate a development strategy and ensure a balanced structure of the product portfolio.

The London Business School maintained in 1985 (LBS, 1985) that 'when good strategic planners and good marketers work well together, the combination is powerful'. Palmer (1998, 48) debates the issue for services marketing:

There can be argument about the relationship between corporate planning and marketing planning. At one extreme the two are seen as synonymous. If an organization stands or falls primarily on its ability to satisfy customer needs, then it can be argued that marketing planning is so central to the organization's activities that it becomes corporate planning. The alternative view is that marketing is just one of the functions of an organization which affects its performance.

Sadly, he appears to be equating marketing with merely promotion in this counter argument.

It is salutary to read the views of executives from giant companies of the past who analyse the failure of corporate planning and who identify that failure as arising because 'corporate management has tended to ignore essential elements of successful business practices, such as implementing marketing analysis and product planning; employing modern equipment, methods and procedures; and establishing quality control' (Dunn and Schuster, 1985, 19).

Marketing's position should be central to all planning processes: it is the heart of knowledge of the marketplace and the source of interpretation of that knowledge, while it also has responsibilities for profit margins, increasing market share and market penetration.

Marketing personnel can create strategies for expansion or diversification, plan maximum competitiveness, create, as well as answer, customer needs, identify new markets and gaps in existing markets, and initiate research and development innovations. (Who would have thought, for example, that the world had a need for an adhesive that did not have permanent sticking properties? Now paper clips are disappearing as 3M's Post-it's™ proliferate.)

'Marketing-driven organizations' are the high-fliers, i.e. the best performers, according to Hooley and Lynch's research survey of 1700 companies (1985). Three characteristics that highfliers displayed to a significant degree (not displayed by the 'also-rans', the companies lagging behind) were:

- genuine marketing orientation
- strategic sensitivity and responsiveness
- profit orientation, rooted in a well-developed sense of marketing assets.

The specific relationship between strategic, corporate planning and marketing needs careful definition and design for each individual organization. There are fundamental questions to be addressed if there is not to be conflict in uncoordinated allocations of human and financial resources:

- Where does marketing fit in the jigsaw of the corporate organization or authority of which the library or information centre is a part?
- How much consultation and participation, and with whom, is required?
- What negotiations are needed?
- What are the reporting mechanisms?

- What resources are there to support the marketing function?
- Who is responsible for resource control and implementation?
- What evaluation procedures and control mechanisms are built in?

Organization size and resource bases will affect the responses of librarians and information professionals to some of these issues, but planning cannot be successful unless it really gets down to the specifics of who is to do what, when, where and how.

> The job of marketing planning is, broadly, to structure the future use of resources, and principally the marketing mix, in order to achieve the objectives, goals or targets which stem from the firm's strategic planning. (Foxall, 1981, 29)

Librarians and information professionals need to appreciate that strategic marketing planning aims at meeting user and customer needs, to ensure that there is a sustainable fit between resources and the present and future marketplace. The step-by-step development of a marketing plan is discussed in Chapter 10.

At the functional level, finance, personnel, service management, and research and development may well be alongside marketing, all interdependent and equally dependent on corporate decisions, but, in turn, the corporate decisions are based on information and advice from the functional level. Roles at functional levels, because of their very interdependence, may in reality cause conflict. Poor internal communications will lead to a longer decision-making process and reduced effectiveness in implementation. Thus, for example, marketing may have its goals, strategies, schedules, costs and personnel amended, or even eroded, by a finance department seeking to provide shareholders with obvious profits or a library committee with obvious savings. It is a corporate responsibility to see that clashes in objectives are avoided. Central direction and co-operative measures will lead to a reduction in such functional conflict. It is said that doing things right is efficiency, but doing the right thing is effectiveness. The organization needs to be structured in such a way as to be flexible enough to be able to do the right thing at the right time, and, in a world attuned to ethical marketing, for the right reasons, as displayed in the mission statement.

Librarians and information professionals need to be aware and acknowledge that even where their organizations have good strategies, they may fail because of poor implementation. Evaluation procedures throughout are vital parts of the strategic plan as a consequence. One of the ways in which such professionals can make a personal impact at the strategic level and influence decisions is to take responsibility for evaluation data and presentation. This is, after all, an information communication function that librarians and information professionals are well qualified to fulfil.

Organizational cultures can change and whether the structure is hierarchy, pyramid, flat or latest model on the market, librarians and information professionals must be principal actors in the change process and add marketing as a role to their already considerable repertoire.

References and further reading

Bate, P. (1995) *Strategies for cultural change*, Butterworth-Heinemann.

Bonoma, T. V. and Clark, B. H. (1988) *Marketing performance assessment*, Harvard Business School Press.

British Library (1993) *The British Library for scholarship, research and innovation; strategic objectives for the year 2000*, The British Library Board.

Chisnall, P. M. (1989) *Strategic industrial marketing*, Prentice Hall.

Dunn, K. L. and Schuster, D. R. (1985) Running the information systems organization like a business, *Information Strategy: the Executives Journal*, **1** (3), 19–23.

Fowler, E. and Graves, P. (1995) *Managing an effective operation*, The Institute of Management Foundation/Butterworth-Heinemann.

Foxall, G. R. (1981) *Strategic marketing management*, Croom Helm.

Haberberg, A. and Rieple, A. (2001) *The strategic management of organisations*, Pearson Education.

Hooley, G. J. and Lynch, J. E. (1985) Marketing lessons from the UK's high-flying companies, *Journal of Marketing Management*, **1** (1), 65–74.

Hooley, G., Lynch, J. and Shepherd, J. (1990) The marketing concept: putting theory into practice, *European Journal of Marketing*, **24** (9), 7–23.

Jobber, D. (2001) *Principles and practice of marketing*, 3rd edn, McGraw-Hill.

Johnson, B. (1999) *Introducing management: a development guide for new managers*, Butterworth-Heinemann.

Lambin, J.-J. (2000) *Market-driven management*, Macmillan Press.

Levitt, T. (1960) Marketing myopia, *Harvard Business Review*, **38** (4), 45–56.

London Business School (1985) Building a market driven company, *Journal*, **10** (1), 22.

Lovelock, C. and Wright, L. (1999) *Principles of service marketing and management*, Prentice Hall.

OAL (1991) Great Britain: Office of Arts and Libraries, *Setting objectives for public library services*, Library Information Series No. 19, OAL.

Palmer, A. (1998) *Principles of service marketing*, 2nd edn, McGraw-Hill; 3rd edn, McGraw-Hill, 2001 .

Peters, T. (1998) *The circle of innovation*, Hodder and Stoughton.

Pirsig, R. (1974) *Zen and the art of motorcycle maintenance*, Bantam Books.

Steffire, V. (1985) *Developing and implementing marketing strategies*, Praeger.

Stewart, R. (1997) *The reality of management*, Butterworth-Heinemann.

Walker, B. in Coles, M. (1993) Marketing industry, *Marketing Business*, (April), 11–13.

Webster, F. (1995) *Theories of the information society*, Routledge.

Wickham, P. A. (2000) *Financial Times corporate strategy casebook*, Pearson Education.

3

MARKETING STRATEGIES FOR LIBRARIANS AND INFORMATION PROFESSIONALS

The essence of marketing strategy for libraries and information services is to identify how they can best grow and become stronger in an increasingly competitive marketplace. The role of strategic marketing is both medium and long term: to lead the library and information service to opportunities in the marketplace, current and potential, to manage the resource base and seek new sources and to aim for successful growth in both existing and new markets.

The objectives of this chapter are:

- to introduce the concepts of marketing audits, PEST and SWOT, via macroenvironmental and microenvironmental scanning
- to show how the library and information service might use portfolio management and product lifecycle theory effectively
- to suggest relevant marketing strategies for libraries and information services.

Strategy development

The mission statement will answer the question 'what business are we in?' and must be implemented via a set of strategies that will satisfy both short- and long-term objectives. The strategic PEST audit, plus the audit of strengths, weaknesses, opportunities and threats, discussed below, provides an analysis of the current situation, external and internal.

Continuous monitoring provides the data to enable forecasts to be made of what is likely to happen over time if present trends and strategies continue. A momentum forecast of this kind, when compared with mission targets, will undoubtedly throw up a measurable gap – the bigger the gap the bigger the need to search out alternative strategies to remedy and close that gap, or revise the mission objectives. Strategies that are likely to lead to a successful outcome will most often be based on client or user satisfaction, which means that the library or information service must continue to ask itself the following questions at regular intervals:

- What business are we in?
- Where should we be?
- What groups should we be serving?
- What user needs must we satisfy?
- What technology will be used to answer those needs?
- What other resources do we need?

These questions answered, or at least tackled, librarians and information professionals can begin to plan their strategies.

Environmental scanning

Identification, analysis and evaluation of the major influences that are likely to affect the future prosperity of the library or information service are prerequisites of any strategic planning. Many standard marketing texts introduce macroenvironmental scanning before discussing mission statements. A mission statement, however, is not cast in stone: it is a point of departure, and the journey proposed, as well as the point of arrival, must be open to change. The rate of change in the post-modern, IT-enabled world is phenomenal and the customer (user, reader, client in the marketplace) is becoming more marketing literate according to research by Baker (2001, 29): 'respondents can deconstruct campaigns using the language of marketing'.

Both the macro-environment and the micro-environment need to be monitored in the successful management of change. Ongoing and continuous environmental scanning is imperative if libraries and information services are to be ahead of the competition and succeed in their objectives.

In the wider macro-environment the uncontrollable variables affecting the library or information service and its markets are complex and dynamic; they are the forces that operate in political, economic, social and cultural and technological contexts. The analysis of these variables is known in marketing jargon as a PEST (from the initial letters of the contexts), although some writers use the less telling description, 'STEP analysis'.

Closer to home and also needing attention are the agencies directly involved, or in competition, with the library or information service; they include suppliers or distributors of information or products who either affect or potentially affect the services offered. There are other variables too that demand monitoring by all librarians and information professionals: demographic factors and trends and the ever increasing burden of relevant legislation.

The ability to gather information, judge its validity and respond accordingly is where librarians and information professionals are already at the cutting edge. Environmental scanning is a service that they can offer to their parent organization as a vital tool in the decision-making process, as well as operating it successfully on behalf of their own service. It is comparatively easy in the commercial sector for information professionals to identify relevant information-indicating trends vital to the work of key personnel in their company. In other sectors, the librarian will need to ascertain that regular information bulletins are not provided already, for example, by information management departments. Where this is the case, the librarian should be considering convergence, merger, takeover, as part of the marketing plan. Information provision and management, wherever it occurs in the organization, should centre on their service. The initiation of such environmental scanning information services, perhaps directly to the vice chancellor's or rector's office in higher education, or to the chief executive in a local authority, is a marketing opportunity to influence key decision makers and their perceptions of library services, with very little outlay in terms of resources as well as a service growth area.

Political and economic trends

Political forces, international, national and local, will have direct or indirect implications for all libraries and information services to varying degrees, because of the pervasive nature of the information world and, naturally, because political factors cannot be divorced from economic, legal and social factors.

A post-industrial society with the emphasis on a service economy and (perhaps enforced) leisure environment has already brought new demands for information services and library provision. Those demands will go on growing and changing as political boundaries change or disappear, and blocs of evolution, not to say revolution, bring about new emphases for education, information working patterns and quality of life.

A computer-literate society is demanding appropriate access points to serve its information needs and it is vital that librarians and information professionals are seen to be in the vanguard of new networking developments. In their study of the public library and the internet, Criddle et al. (2000, 232) conclude: 'What's next – collaboration, both geographically and across sectors in a networked environment, is not only possible but desirable. Joining together and sharing information reduces the duplication of resources and effort. Integrating effort and content from a variety of sources has the potential to create wide-ranging network resources of major significance.'

Skills shortages, now worldwide, suggest that there is a need for academic and public libraries alike to provide support services to those embarking on retraining or re-entering a country's workforce. Small and medium enterprises, said to be an integral part of the economic way forward, need all the support and information nourishment that libraries and information services can so ably supply. New trading blocs have provided fruitful niche marketing for legal information services, and there is enormous potential for other library and information services in the hotbed of cultural differences. When new businesses set up, opportunities for providing commercial business information are self-evident, but the public librarian might also like to consider providing on-the-spot education and leisure materials for the employees of such companies. Organizations, large and small, are seeking to become learning organizations and there is a marketing opportunity here to be exploited by information professionals to provide training and development, as well as resources, within and external to the organization. Mobile libraries visit rural areas – could not public and academic libraries visit business parks and industrial estates too?

In areas where unemployment is high, the public library will need to expand its community service role and provide more services attuned to the needs of the unemployed, both newly unemployed and long-term. Public libraries can co-operate closely with local education institutions, as well as providing complementary open- and distance-learning materials. Public libraries in the UK are in the vanguard of government developments aiming at 'making the UK one of the world's leading knowledge economies' (Howarth, 2001). Library staff are being trained as part of an information and communications technology training network funded under the New Opportunities Funding programme advised by Resource (the Council for Museums, Archives and Libraries). Howarth (2001) says: 'By the end of 2002 we expect all 3,500 public library service points in England to have an ICT learning centre, and all will be eligible to gain the UK Online branding.'

Demographic trends affect all libraries: in education sectors, school, college and university libraries feel the knock-on effect of falling birth rates. Public libraries will need to prepare for a much-enlarged older population in the next 20 years and, moreover, for what are likely to be very much changed needs from that sector of the population. The University of the Third Age is already in existence and silver surfers are a substantial proportion of the confident internet user market. A company information centre also will watch demographic trends closely – a fall or rise in the birth rate will affect the health of the information unit just as sharply as the rest of the company, if the company makes child products and new markets must be sought. Johnson and Johnson, for example, have famously responded to this potential threat by emphasizing the gentle nature of their baby products, shampoo, and so on; in a world more aware and wary of harsh chemical ingredients, they have successfully entered a completely new adult market.

Climatic monitoring will also be an essential part of the job for the information officer in industry, where his or her company is dependent on raw materials or particular distribution routes. Other markets will need to be sought if, for example, crops are doomed to failure or transport routes disrupted or destroyed. The natural climate has the potential to be as catastrophic as the political climate to many companies and organizations.

Social trends

Economic trends and social trends are inextricably linked with demographic trends. Housing associations are revitalizing run-down city centre areas to provide homes for the expanding single, independent market, and in-fill developments are changing dramatically the character of many areas. New housing developments on the outskirts of towns and cities attract young couples, who bring in their wake, and comparatively quickly, a new child population. Public libraries will need to reassess the location of their branches and their opening hours to serve the needs of these changing patterns of population. Such developments and trends can be mapped with little difficulty since planning departments of local authorities and estate agents are fruitful sources of information. These same estate agents will be pleased to distribute library publicity too, since they are keen to stress the facilities offered in an area that makes their properties more attractive. Another reason to visit the planning department is that new infrastructures and consequent patterns of public transport and public movements and habits can completely alter access to, and use of, library services.

An analysis of trends in leisure activities will point to areas of stock that need to be developed. The increasing number of people taking holidays abroad to destinations ever further flung is an example here. These travellers have a need for information on the countries to be visited, their culture, climate or health risks. Such visits engender a need for further information on the travellers' return, as interest continues in food, wine, music and literature.

Physical environment and climate also need monitoring as part of the macroenvironment scan. The greening of organizations is a literal as well as a philosophical phenomenon in libraries and information services, as green bins for waste paper appear almost everywhere. Users have different expectations and information needs in this connection today. Marketing strategies should include serving those needs and enhancing the library or information service's own image as an organization genuinely caring about the environment.

In a multicultural context, community leaders can advise on behaviour patterns that might affect the delivery of information and library services. It may be that a greater provision of own-language or dual-language materials would be useful, but very often an initial step is to provide a comfortable, welcoming meeting place where, gradually, real needs can be investigated in a supportive group atmosphere. Organizations and companies with an international scope of activities or where a workforce includes a diversity of cultural backgrounds need to ensure that such diversity is catered for in all the organization's communications, and information services must reflect this approach too, including any promotion materials. Beware, for example, the too facile use of clip-art programmes, which rarely demonstrate an awareness of a world rich in diversity. A well-known international company with strong equal opportunities policies and real recognition of, for example, staff religious needs, fell down on something as simple in communication terms as a poster on safety information showing only white faces. The company paid the price in expensive litigation.

It is difficult to obtain robust data on a continuing basis from small groups in a community; access, uncertainty and suspicion of motives can cloud the issues. One researcher, worried why her seemingly innocent questionnaire on attitudes to information services was being rejected by the Chinese population in the UK, found that they suspected her of being a spy from the Inland Revenue.

The literature on socio-cultural studies, both theoretical and empirical, can provide useful background material on processes and changes in evolutionary, historical and genetic dynamics. It cannot replace vital market research and communication with the clients and users of the library or information service, which will identify concerns and influences on their expectations and behaviour.

Cultural traditions and values have affected libraries in strangely contrasting ways. Most parts of the world have experienced nightmare floods in recent years (and this trend is not likely to disappear), but the way the world reacted to save the libraries of Italy was in complete contrast with the way that libraries were treated in Bangladesh. All available relief in the latter-named country went to health, hospitals, road rebuilding and education, and there was no programme for rebuilding the libraries.

Technology trends

The ever accelerating changes in technology, affecting clients and users as well as library and information services, are well chronicled everywhere and discussed further in Chapter 7 'Marketing in the digital age'. Trends in technology have been ignored too often in the past. Overload of information gives the problem of attempting to sort the vital from the merely interesting, not to mention the hyperbole and chaff.

Naisbitt and Aberdene (1982; 1990) forecast a world of small communities, where the home would be the centre of work and leisure activities, linked to the outside world by electronic networks, but where the specialist professional or craftsman would find a niche. In the 21st century, the laptop is already making way for the palm-held computer, hot desking is giving way to no physical contact with the office at all, surgeons are operating via computer monitors and students are at a distance on flexible learning programmes. Where does the library or information centre fit in this scenario?

In 1993 the British Library Dainton Lecture on High Performance Libraries explored the premise that the library's traditional role as acquirer, organizer and provider of recorded knowledge was to be broadened and reinterpreted by the rapid increase in electronic knowledge sources of many kinds. Dr Donald Lindberg, delivering the lecture, maintained that:

> Advances in computer design, fabrication, and marketing of information systems make even more urgent society's needs for the library. The broader social effects of these technologies could be positive, for instance, by facilitating telecommut-

ing or assisting physically disabled workers. But without better national systems of education and training, many citizens may be disenfranchised observers of the bewildering changes which stem from electronic information processing.

Is the training coming too late, despite his early warning, to ensure that librarians are major players?

Professionals work from home, and home leisure facilities have boomed: satellite television, sophisticated video and audio equipment, computer games, home gymnasia and health-checking devices are common. One can shop from home and bank from home via telephone, television and the internet. In Europe, July 2001 saw UK legislation on the acceptance of digital signatures and Spain has seen the acceptance of digital signatures as legal as wet signatures via Infomarket, a web-based commercial service, for some time. The electronic cottage is here and functioning effectively; who needs to 'go to the library'?

The huge demand for telephone information services began the trend to leave libraries behind. It is possible, at a price, to ring for information on areas as diverse as alimony and zinc deficiency: health, sex, baby weaning, gardening, law, motoring, pop music – the list is endless, but it does reflect what might traditionally have been called the subject catalogue. Why then did libraries not achieve greater volume of use? Is it that the presentation of information, packaged in easily accessible nuggets – look up your problem or symptoms, ring this number – seems so much simpler in comparison to the mystique of the numerology of Dewey? Are the impersonal tones of the answering services preferred to the friendly, or unfriendly, librarian or information professional?

The internet, via home, office or WAP mobile telephone, is achieving exponential user growth. The fingertip information may be too much, inaccurate, from untried or corrupt sources, but it's there and easily accessible. Student, researcher, parent in a panic – for them it is often the first, and too often the only, source of information sought.

How many libraries or information services advertise direct telephone numbers for their specialist staff? How many libraries or information services are actively informing and educating their users, readers and clients about information credibility?

Environmental scanning provides the potential to identify marketing opportunities as well as the context for strategic planning.

The marketing audit – SWOT analysis

The essence of marketing strategy for libraries and information services is to identify how they can best grow and become stronger in an increasingly competitive marketplace. A strategic audit of the library or information service's strengths, weaknesses, opportunities and threats will provide an analysis of the situation, external and internal.

This analysis of strengths, weaknesses, opportunities and threats (SWOT analysis) is sometimes a difficult procedure for librarians and information professionals, so used are they to serving others and working under constraints, that it takes them some time to recognize strengths and opportunities, although they are only too eager to identify weaknesses and threats. It is important to remember that once a weakness is identified, steps can be taken to remedy it, through staff training or whatever may be required, so that potentially it could become a strength.

Strengths might include staff, stock, services and physical location, but these are just as likely to be weaknesses in some organizations, so there are no neat checklists or guidelines. It is important to emphasize what is uniquely special about the particular library or information service and, in effect, identify what it can do that the competition cannot. Services might be intangible, but they very often have a visible face, and good staff–client staff–user relationships are paramount in maintaining a quality service. An information service offering an extensive range of databases may be weakened by not having enough telephone lines to serve users' needs; a constantly engaged line is a sign of an organization in crisis. What then needs to be considered? What can be marketed, what might support the marketing effort and what might be a constraint? Here follow some suggestions.

SWOT analysis can identify strengths that should be maintained to provide quality services. Knowledge sharing, the mantra of the 21st century, is often seen as a threat by individuals who perceive their knowledge and information as defining their role in the organization and sometimes in life. It can affect staff in all areas of a library's business and in every facet of information services. Library and information managers need to market the concept of knowledge sharing to their own staff and then to all members of the organization. Sharing knowledge of *how to share knowledge*, with the strength of a lifetime of information sharing to give credibility, will promote the professional skills of the librarian and information professional. It can be an opportunity to take the lead and direct operations. Librarians in the public sector may ask how this might apply to their situation. They need to look to the size and complexity of the authorities of which they are a part and if their marketing skills are exercised they will become an integral part of the authority with their expert knowledge respected and needed. How many public libraries are the driving force behind on-street electronic information points or tourism information services? When they are, do their publics know that they are responsible? Are they given credit for these very public-face services that add extra value for the community? Obvious examples, yes, but who forges the links between planning officials, social services departments, leisure programmes, health information in the community, education activities, lifelong learning initiatives? Who could be at the nub of the network?

Threats, real and perceived, can be turned to marketing opportunities. The move of a research department to a different geographical location or the removal of senior management from expensive capital city headquarters pose an obvious threat to the information service and its relationships. A merger or buyout, similarly, could pose a huge threat. These situations should be used as an opportunity to reassess services offered, to prove added value in a time of change, demonstrate through an active and continuous presence a variety of services. Personnel on the move are often disgruntled and insecure, or they may be optimistic and looking to new challenges. Either way, providing them with relevant information at the right time and in the right format will prove the value of the information service. This information does not necessarily have to be commercial information only. Information about schools for their children can be as vital as product information when provided at the right time, and will add to the number of those who will act as champions for the information service. It is important that senior management and key decision makers know about the information centre's activities. Executives who leave are an expensive drain on any organization; keep them happy instead and the Chair, Board and Chief Executive Officer will be happy with the information centre. It's good public relations and a threat has been used as an opportunity.

A SWOT analysis done in consultation with service staff will often produce interesting responses. The gap in perceptions between senior managers and their staff as to what are strengths and what are weaknesses will usually surprise the staff less than the managers and emphasizes the need for collective ownership of the marketing effort through internal communication.

Portfolio management

Portfolio management looks at the whole picture of an organization and how individual products and services contribute to the overall health of the organization, even though they may be managed on an individual basis. The librarian or information professional needs to decide, for example, how strong services might support weaker services, if they should support them, or whether new services can be developed even further which might replace declining services.

The concept of portfolio management, as part of strategic planning, is particularly attractive from a marketing perspective. The various elements within an organization's activities can be managed effectively with separate, albeit perhaps complementary, marketing mixes. The concept of the marketing mix is discussed in detail in Chapter 4.

There are many models of portfolio analysis in the business world; the growth-share model of the highly reputable Boston Consulting Group (BCG) has been selected for discussion here. Others include the Arthur D. Little strategic condition matrix, the General Electric Market Attractiveness-Competitive Position (MA-CP) model with McKinsey and Co and the

Shell directional policy matrix, all discussed in varying detail in major marketing texts. Jobber (2001) in particular is recommended for the clear explanations, plus the select criticisms, of portfolio management presented.

The Boston Consulting Group model analyses the various products of a business on a matrix that measures relative market share and the rate of market growth. It is necessary to consider what is likely to happen in the market, i.e. potential growth, and to examine the competitive position very closely. Librarians and information professionals can use the conceptual framework of the model without necessarily involving themselves in the logarithmic scales of market share and growth. In the modern world of performance assessment, competitive tendering and so on, the model is a practical working tool. It is a tool that must be used in conjunction with an analysis of the broader trends identified via environmental scanning and the data produced by the library or information service marketing information system.

The BCG matrix model (see Figure 3.1) requires that the organization divides its activities into operational areas known as strategic business units (SBUs) with a view to making strategic decisions about the relative health, resources needed, risks to be taken and activities to be discontinued.

The library/information service portfolio

The classification of the small business units (SBUs) or activities of the library or information service will cause debate, healthy in itself because it will generate the need for management to think about services strategically and examine the integrative nature of SBUs. The BCG model uses the classifiers Cash Cows, Question Marks, Stars and Dogs (see Figure 3.1).

STARS	QUESTION MARKS
CASH COWS	DOGS

Fig. 3.1 *An adaptation of the BCG portfolio analysis matrix*

Cash Cows are the income generators for a business, needing little in the way of new resources. These are well-established activities with a large share of the market and providing consistent and substantial profits. In the library world one could translate this into the services which receive most support from users, although increasingly libraries are as much in need of cash–profit generators as their counterparts in business and industry where it is not enough to be merely cost effective.

Question Marks are activities where potential is very high, but demand for resources in terms of equipment, personnel and finance is also high and competition probably intense. The obvious contender for classification in this category for most information services would be web activities. The decision to be made is challenging: resource the activity at a high level, stay in the game and be prepared to keep on pouring resources in, in the hope of future gain, or pull out before the organization or other activities are disadvantaged. A substantial decrease in libraries' use of CD-ROM services in comparison with online emphasizes the need for such decisions.

BCG's *Stars* are usually former Question Marks; the organization will have become a market leader where this product or service is concerned. However, caution is needed here too: a Star may not necessarily be a highly profitable activity and it may need considerable resources to keep in the lead. The amount of publicity, goodwill and acclaim generated by a library providing extensive IT hardware and software or multiple copies of the top ten novels, discs and video tapes to satisfy the users might keep it ahead in the competitive world, but is the drain on the other services worth while? The online access to medical databases offered by a university library may appear to be ruinously expensive, but in terms of likely support in funding battles and a potential fee-generating activity, it will be essential to continue. Provided the leading edge is maintained, the service should become a *Cash Cow*.

BCG would have the *Dogs* shot. These are the areas that generate little activity, low profit or even losses; market share is low in a low- or no-growth market. Unless there is potential for expansion in the future, or a competitor is disadvantaged by continuation of the service, a decision needs to be made to cut that service or divest the organization of it.

Most SBUs, or areas of activity, will follow a lifecycle pattern of Question Mark, Star, Cash Cow, Dog, so it is as well to review the portfolio continually. This leads to better control mechanisms, more efficient information being collected on services and activities and, often, creative thinking. There is nothing like putting a service under threat, in the Dogs category or that of Question Mark, to have ideas generated for potential growth in that area. Worldwide, millennium headlines were ousted when Heinz announced the dropping of salad cream from their product range. The tabloids sought out celebrities who swore they could not live without it, supermarket shelves emptied as the threatened withdrawal date grew near and the decision was rescinded as the outcry from the public – and the size of Heinz profits – grew. Recently, when threatened with removal in a similar fashion, music resources in a UK public library underwent a resurgence of interest and started to break lending records.

Each library or information centre will, no doubt, be able to invent equally expressive descriptions for the Boston classifications to analyse current and potential strategy. The BCG matrix has achieved classic status as a model; it has many imitators and attempts to reinvent its categories are legion. One of the more recent, couched in today's technology terms, is that of Gabay (2000, 22–4). He translates cash cows in cyberspace into 'Satellites', mature market operations with much internet traffic. Stars are 'Supernovas'; he gives the example of the popular search engine, Yahoo!. Gabay's 'Comets' are BCG's Question Marks, websites with all the latest enhancements. 'Black Holes' are the equivalent of Dogs, surfers will only skim these sites and the message is clear they need to disappear.

Product and market strategies

The classic product/market matrix that Igor Ansoff (1957) suggested (see Figure 3.2 on page 45) is to be found in all marketing texts. As a framework for considering strategies it appeals to management because it aids the assessment of, and planning for, growth potential. Librarians and information professionals can adopt and adapt it with ease to suit their purposes.

The initial consideration, *market penetration strategy*, is an examination of whether current users could be encouraged to make greater or more frequent use of existing services. Many existing users are unaware of the range of services offered or might be persuaded to become more regular users. There will be potential users who match the profile of existing users, i.e. they are in the same market, who might be persuaded of the benefits of existing services.

It is usually more cost effective to work with existing users, and the possibilities of converting them to other services are greater, so this is an obvious starting point. The effectiveness of data mining and user–customer relationship management, discussed in Chapter 7, are prime factors in operating this strategy sucesfully.

Market research will provide information on user profiles, levels of awareness, benefits claimed in using the services, etc., and this will form the basis of promotional strategies.

Current services may well prove attractive to clients who are different from the existing users – *market development strategy*. A college library might consider opening its services to the local community. A company's information centre might consider a new geographical area: while Europe is already targeted, what about the explosion of development on the Pacific Rim?

Service development strategy will call for creative thinking: how can existing services be enhanced? A faster turnaround on periodical article or interlibrary loan provision, with use of telephone or e-mail to say an item has arrived? A difference in opening hours at service points or the introduction of technology to benefit readers? More comfortable seating in reading areas, extra photocopying or fax facilities, more telephone lines, internet access points, refreshment services, lavatories and baby feeding and changing facilities? Records managers can provide relevant data to aid in identifying other opportunities to develop services offered. Health and sickness records can identify company employees' needs for information on preventative health measures or stress management at key dates in the year. Presented with actuarial dates re mortality rates for male executives and employees who are allowing poor diet, too little exercise and too much alcohol consumption to reduce their lifespan, an organization will welcome more and continual

	Current services/products	New services/products
Current markets	Market penetration	Service/product development
New markets	Market development	Diversification

Fig. 3.2 *An adaptation of H. I. Ansoff's Product–Market Development Strategy Matrix*

information from the information centre on reversing the trend.

Diversification entails the greatest risk since it involves entering unknown waters. Concentric diversification strategy is often the most attractive since it requires the organization to seek out developments that have some kind of synergy with existing practices. A library is efficient in organizing the collection and lending of materials: might it consider entering the formal dress-hire business and appeal to a completely new clientele? There are a number of successful video rental business owners and record shop managers who were librarians in previous reincarnations. Thus the question to ask is, what are we good at? Followed by, can our skills be applied successfully elsewhere? Creative thinking should be high on the list of attributes of librarians and information professionals. The mileage for public libraries in foreign travel is unlimited: information on foreign lands and cultures in book and periodical form, rooms for viewing videos or foreign films, carrels and audiovisual equipment for learning a language, online facilities capable of contacting airline and other travel operators as well as national tourist offices direct.

With staff whose professional specialities include evaluating information as well as organizing client records commissions could be rolling in. But how many opportunities have been missed? Large health authorities with massive IT infrastructures, systems and personnel are effective organizers of information, but where do local health centres or primary care groups obtain knowledge and advice in reorganizing their paper records into electronic format? Librarians sadly lost out to the commercial world in the market potential for cataloguing and displaying visual material. Omnivex, Inc. combined videodisk and computing technologies in an indexing and retrieval system now being used by art galleries and museums worldwide. Could a group of librarians not have done the same?

Horizontal diversification strategy entails looking for opportunities that might very well provide benefit to existing users, but that are unrelated to existing practices. Thus a school library or university library might consider setting up table tennis or billiard facilities in the reading rooms or, more likely, a newsagent's or stationery shop on the premises.

Conglomerate diversification strategy concerns the identification of opportunities that bear no relationship to existing markets, services or practices, the sort of opportunities that would never have been considered by librarians or information professionals in the past. The need would not have been there, but just as local management of schools in the UK forced a reconsideration of perceptions, so must managers in the library and information world be prepared for new pressures and look for new ways forward.

The Ansoff model demands careful analysis of the current situation and markets. Technology access and expertise is vital for today's markets to be served effectively and librarians and information professionals must focus on quality service.

Ansoff's model also asks for creativity and innovation. Although some of the world's innovations we can do without – training shoes which twinkle for example – libraries and information services must be seen to be part of today's world. Librarians and information professionals must demonstrate that they are attuned to a 21st-century, caring, nurturing New Age. Libraries and information centres should be 'egg shaped' in a 21st century where everything else is, demonstrated in the curvature of the products around us: furniture, motor cars, pens, television sets, DVD players, mobile phones. Company logos are oval shaped as they are revamped, new architectural structures arch and curve; the rotunda of the new Sackler Library for Oxford University is a beautiful example. Nurturing, new age, rebirth, are the semiotics of the new century: these are not design fads but reflect inner needs and drives. Doctors came out from behind their desks long ago to sit side by side with their patients, removing barriers, creating new, caring relationships; sadly librarians and information professionals are doing the opposite and hiding behind self-service issue systems.

The library or information centre cannot rebuild, refit or refurbish as often as commercial sectors, and taking hacksaws to library furniture is not recommended. Users can, however, be *nurtured*. Notices and fonts can be rounded in format. Information specialists can come out from their closets, real or perceived. Water machines (and what shape are they?) can be placed in convenient locations. Communications can be couched in less formal language and users can receive relevant communications more often, utilizing today's technologies. A culture of creativity must be part of the marketing strategy; librarians and information professionals need to think creatively and think success.

Product lifecycle

The product lifecycle concept is helpful in deciding which marketing strategies are best fitted to particular stages in the development of service activities. Product lifecycle theory maintains that all products or services follow distinctive patterns over time. The stages in the product lifecycle curve are Introduction, Growth, Maturity, Decline, the time period within stages differing according to type of product or service (see Figure 3.3). The product lifecycle curve is not in itself a predictor, but it can be an effective aid to marketing planning. One could ascribe the theory to, for example, the whole of library history or the development of CD-ROMS in information services. It is an attractive device to add to portfolio management techniques in assessing the relative position of services. Many writers have suggested further sophisticated stages, such as Turbulence, Saturation and Petrification, but the four basic stages serve management well in decision making.

Fig. 3.3 *Product lifecycle curve*

The introduction of any new service or product will be a difficult time. Resources are being expended on an area that will probably have an initially slow take-up rate by users. A deliberate rapid penetration strategy can be implemented to help, but this involves massive spending on promotion and incentive strategies, which makes sense only if the user market is a large one and unaware of the service. User awareness and acceptance will take the service into a growth stage, which will eventually plateau out into a maturity stage as most of the market for the service settles into a regular pattern of use. The need to identify the point before maturity creeps into decline is paramount. It is at this point that innovation and new marketing strategies need to be implemented if the service is to revive and possibly take off into a growth curve again.

A glance at supermarket shelves will show sales being regenerated by new, improved, enhanced, repackaged products. In the library or information service, different staff, redeployed from other geographical or specialist areas, can rejuvenate a service at the maturity stage. Moving stock around within a location can generate interest. Exhibitions, displays and events can highlight a service and attract new users. A new website can regenerate interest in a service.

Carrying out market research on a service can remind users of neglected aspects. An advertised telephone answering service or interactive website can inject new vitality, and by monitoring the type and timing of queries additional information on the potential use of the service is garnered. Other examples of opportunities for revitalization might be areas of stock in, say, a university library, where a previously strong course is diminishing in student numbers, or where specific periodical titles, highly topical and extensively used previously, are now of limited value. Are these Dogs or are there other potential users for these expensive resources in other faculties?

The product lifecycle concept should be used in a context of experience and known variables, since the period of each stage varies among products and services, and even types of industry. The product lifecycle is affected by the nature of the product or service, changes in the macro- and microenvironments, changes in the user profile and the introduction of competition.

When evaluating user opinions on a service in order to identify its position in the product lifecycle, it is also wise to consider user adoption characteristics. The opinions of those who are receptive to new ideas and willing to be the first to try new products or services will be vastly different from those who would rather wait and see, or those who are always the last to try anything. The marketing concept that describes user behaviour in this respect is known as *diffusion of innovation*, and user behaviour from Innovators to Early Adopters to Laggards is discussed in Chapter 6 'Market segmentation'.

Librarians and information professionals will find the implementation of marketing audits, PEST and SWOT, no problem when it comes to collecting the information on trends. The consulting processes in the production of a SWOT will undoubtedly be less easy, and produce surprises, and certainly the application of a portfolio analysis will generate debate. Ansoff's matrix and the examination of product–service lifecycles will produce more surprises and more creativity: welcome it.

References and further reading

Ansoff, H. I. (1957) Strategies for diversification, *Harvard Business Review*, **25** (5), 113–24.

Baker, S. (2001) Welcome to the future, *Marketing Business*, (September), 28–31.

Coulter, M. (2002) *Strategic management in action*, 2nd edn, Prentice Hall.

Criddle, S. et al. (2000) *The public librarian's guide to the internet*, Library Association Publishing in association with the Office for Library and Information Networking.

Ensor, J. (2001) *Strategic marketing management: planning and control*, Butterworth-Heinemann/The Chartered Institute of Marketing.

Gabay, J. J. (2000) *Successful cybermarketing*, Hodder and Stoughton.

Howarth, A. (2001) Building the new age together, *Library Association Record*, **103** (5), 266.

Jobber, D. (2001) *Principles and practice of marketing*, 3rd edn, McGraw-Hill.

Kilbourne, W. E. and Beckmann, S. C. (1998) Review and critical assessment of research on marketing and the environment, *Journal of Marketing Management*, **14** (6), 513–32.

Lambin, J.-J. (2000) *Market-driven management: strategic and operational marketing*, Macmillan Press.

Lindberg, D. (1993) *High performance libraries* (Dainton Lecture), British Library.

Naisbitt, J. and Aberdene, P. (1982) *Megatrends: ten new directions transforming our lives*, Warner Books.

Naisbitt, J. and Aberdene, P. (1990) *Megatrends 2000*, Sidgwick and Jackson.

Oldroyd, M. (2001) *Marketing environment*, Butterworth-Heinemann/The Chartered Institute of Marketing.

Piercy, N. (2001) *Market-led strategic change*, 3rd edn, Butterworth-Heinemann.

4
THE MARKETING MIX

The marketing mix is the planned package of elements that makes up the product or service offered to the market. It is aimed at supporting the library and information service to reach target markets and specified objectives.

The key issues to consider are user convenience, user cost and user communication; taking core services and packaging them according to the needs of specific user groups is a priority.

The objectives of this chapter are:

- to define marketing mix for librarians and information professionals
- to outline the nature of the elements of the marketing mix
- to discuss the traditional 4Ps of the marketing mix: product, place, price and promotion
- to introduce 4Cs as more appropriate for libraries and information services: user considerations, user cost, user convenience and user communication.

The marketing mix is a key concept in marketing, but it needs to be understood thoroughly before strategic decisions are made on its applications.

Is it the magic formula that will put all to rights, whatever the organization, whatever its problems? No, like all marketing concepts and techniques the marketing mix is an integral part of marketing planning that depends on environmental scanning, market research, understanding users, readers and clients, and offering quality products and services. But it is a substantial part of effective marketing strategy, designed to cover all the aspects of the product or service that are important to the customer, or user: how does it answer user needs? Is it attractive? Easy to access? Is it marketed at the right price?

The marketing mix helps to position the library or information service very firmly in the perceptions of their communities served: the wider community for the public library, academic community for the academic library or the clients and customers for the business or specialist information service. Marketing mix needs more properly to be termed marketing mixes, to encourage librarians and information managers to perceive the value of different marketing mixes for specific market segments or groups of users.

Marketing mix elements each have a number of controllable facets or variables tuned to specific markets and the markets for libraries and information services vary enormously. This is why the various elements of the marketing mix are considered at greater length later in this chapter and promotion and public relations discussed in the following chapter.

It is vital to remember that a marketing mix will change over time in accordance with shifts in the macro- and microenvironments, with changes in market segment characteristics (market segmentation is discussed in Chapter 6) and as and when the library or information centre's own vision changes.

The four Ps

The consideration of the interaction of Product, Price, Place and Promotion provides a valuable structure in working towards a set of strategies. When this is coupled with substantial market information and used against a background of careful analysis of the micro- and macro-environment then marketing objectives are more likely to be achieved:

- *Product* – all the product or service characteristics aimed at the target market
- *Price* – the real cost to the customer or user, including other costs than solely money

- *Place* – everywhere and every way the product or service is made available
- *Promotion* – all the methods of communication used to reach the target markets.

McCarthy's (1978) classic model of the four Ps – how the product or service is best presented, in attributes, price, availability and promotion, to the desired market segment – is a development of a theory put forward initially by Neil Borden (1965). Borden's mix is now more precisely found in market research and market strategy.

Librarians and information professionals will need to know that extra 'P's have been added to marketing mix considerations for service marketing:

- *People* – the people who play a part in service delivery
- *Physical evidence* – the environment for service delivery and any tangible representation such as brochures or delivery vehicles
- *Process* – the activities by which the service is delivered.

For those new to marketing, these aspects are already implicit in every facet of the existing four Ps. It is not particularly helpful to seek to pigeon-hole all marketing mix elements in this way but they are useful reminders of what might be considered.

The four Cs

The strategic change and approaches implied by Kotler's four Cs will be a more readily acceptable mix to many librarians and information professionals, who should nevertheless examine both marketing mix formulas closely.

Philip Kotler, the 'experts' expert of marketing', says that marketing must focus more sharply on the customer. He convincingly argued that the seller's paradigm of the four Ps – product, price, place and promotion – should become the four Cs of a buyer's or customer's mix as propounded by Robert Lauterborn (1990) in an interview with Mazur (1991–2). Kotler's name is truly synonymous with marketing. The fact that just about every student and practitioner of marketing has studied and benefited from his work is a testament to his contribution to marketing thinking and practice.

In a customer-oriented marketing mix, product becomes value to the client or user, i.e. customer value; price becomes cost to the customer and includes time and energy cost; place for the customer is convenience and promotion becomes communication. Librarians and information professionals will, therefore, be looking to a marketing mix addressing:

- customer (user) value
- user convenience
- user cost
- user communication.

Some might argue that this is a mere play on words, but it does portray a massive shift in marketing management thinking, philosophy and strategy. The issue is not what words are used but what is the best way to offer value to the user. The marketing mix elements that the library or information service controls 'can be used to satisfy or communicate with customers' (Zeithaml and Bitner, 2000, 18). Interestingly, the customer charters that are now proliferating are also examples of a paradigm shift toward customer satisfaction as a priority.

Creating the marketing mix

The marketing mix is not, as some writers misleadingly state, akin to a recipe, for say a cake, implying that the ingredients work in stated amounts in proportion to each other to produce a predictable outcome. The essential elements of the marketing mix must all be present, but in relation to the specific library or information service, to individual products and services, to the organization and its services at different times, the emphases in parts of the mix will differ accordingly.

Influence of the parent organization on marketing mixes

The markets for libraries and information services are profoundly affected by how elements of the marketing mix – price, place and promotion – are handled for the organization as a whole. To use an analogy, the soft drink manufacturer offers a range of products and services, just as the library or information service does. The markets will be diverse and often complex for each product or service, but the response to those products and services will be affected according to different market segments' perception of the overall organization. When a new soft drink is launched, diet style or vitamin enriched, in new bottles or Tetrapak, via supermarkets or expensive fitness clubs, it is brought to the market in the light, or shade, of its parent company's image and reputation.

Marketing something entirely new is very much easier than attempting to change a target market's indifference to an existing service or to erase a poor image and replace it with a more attractive, exciting service. Take the public library and its education services for instance: how education services are used will depend on how the library is perceived by different market segments. Is it a quality organization, high-technology, budget-conscious, high-performance – or old-fashioned? The public library is expected to offer education materials and services to a massive range of market segments: the under-fives, via their parents; schoolchildren; college and university students, rising numbers of mature students; part-time and evening-class students who are learning for pleasure; distance-learning students to whom the library building becomes their proxy educational institution; the unemployed who wish to retrain; women returning to work; the third age, living longer and making new demands on community services in enhancing their quality of life; local businesses operating in-house training courses. A marketing mix for each group served will have to be designed, but each of the target groups will already have a perception of the public library or the local authority. The marketing mix must take this into account and all the target markets need investigation with this in mind.

What proportion of potential users is being attracted? How satisfied are they with services? Who are the non-users and what are their reasons for nonuse? What changes might be made to provide more effective services? And how might products be augmented? Appropriate levels of materials; changes to loan periods; more comfortable study areas; staff attuned to a different way of treating requests for help; and a system to allow staff to offer a greater quality service in terms of time and depth: all these would be possibilities in the marketing mix. The target markets' attitudes to the parent organization can either make for a receptive audience or a hostile one, and it is in this context that research should be conducted, results considered and a marketing mix designed.

Car manufacturing may provide interesting scenarios for librarians or information professionals to consider. The car manufacturer is not divorced from the specific model in customer's mental maps when choosing a car. It is vital that the company maintains a high profile and quality reputation. The customer perception of the reputation of the car manufacturer will have a huge bearing on choice. The company will be known for its levels of quality, reliability, durability, budget pricing, design flair, high technology or environmental concern. The specific model will be judged against that background and selected or rejected initially because of that perception. Some car manufacturers have had to fight hard to live down past reputations for old-fashioned design, rust corrosion or lack of spare parts; they have, however, managed to revive interest in their vastly improved products.

How might this help the librarian and information professional? The library or information service must also be seen as a quality organization offering a range of appropriate and effective products and services. Renault, Ford and Toyota work as hard on their corporate image – networks of dealerships, staff training, promotion work, after-sales service and the like – as they do on the technical and aesthetic qualities of their individual car models. How many, even of our specialist information services, contact users to discuss whether they have problems that need addressing or merely to check that they are satisfied with current levels of service?

Corporate image management is a vital foundation, and librarians and information professionals will often find they need to win this battle first.

Product and service/Customer value

Kotler (1984, 463) offered the following definition of product: 'A product is anything that can be offered to a market for attention, acquisition, use, or consumption that might satisfy a want or need. It includes physical objects, services, persons, places, organizations, and ideas.' In 2000 (394), he added *information*:

> A **product** is anything that can be offered to a market to satisfy a want or need. Products that are marketed include *physical goods, services, experiences, events, persons, places, properties, organizations, information, and ideas.*

What can be marketed and many of the products and services offered by libraries and information services are discussed in Chapter 1. The message is: *product or service is anything that the library or information service is offering, or could offer, that would be of benefit to users and potential users.*

Services and products offered must present value to the user, over and above actual cost. The design and quality of services are manifest in tangible factors such as timely, up-to-date, appropriate formats, and implicit in intangibles such as staff motivation and training, effective use of resources, and knowledge of user and client needs. The product line can be offered differently from different market segments. Hotel chains offer different types of hotel and service levels for a range of market segments; car models or pens are offered from basic function to super de-luxe model. If this seems far removed from libraries and information services, there are school library services in the UK and USA offering gold-, silver- and bronze-level services according to subscription paid.

Information services in industry and commerce are today managing information resources and focusing on users, on the information requirements of their individual clients. Their product is knowledge and their services knowledge management and knowledge sharing. Their product is truly competitive intelligence, a hugely valuable resource and driver in any company.

The same process can be seen happening in university libraries, which now often treat their undergraduate population differently from post-graduate students in lending services, interlibrary loans and access facilities.

Look again at car manufacturers. They produce a range of models to suit the needs of different market segments from small economical models to top-of-the-range performance cars. Within each model there will be specifications and features to attract buyers. A basic, small, economical model will offer bright colours with lots of trims and a zippy image for the younger market. The same model may suit mothers, who will look for safety, reliability, washability, sturdiness, interior covers and childproof locks. The retired buyer may be looking for a car to reduce running and maintenance costs and will consider the same model. Moving through the product range there will be cars for the family, for the business executive, the speed-seeker and the luxury lover.

Each group will be looking for a different set of characteristics or benefits from what is basically the same form of transport. The manufacturer must offer the most effective package – the additional benefits or services that augment the product – to meet those needs. Features offered, whether as standard or optional, will help the manufacturer to differentiate the company's products from those of the competition. This is especially desirable in a market where it is difficult to produce something really original and where the concept of *unique selling proposition* (features unique to the particular product or service) is not likely to apply very often.

The analogy of car manufacture can also help when it comes to thinking of ways to make the product more attractive overall. The customer will be looking for benefits, tangible benefits yes, but also, and perhaps unconsciously, intangibles. Colour, a tangible feature, is a safety factor: according to motor accident research, some colours make a car disappear in poor light or bad weather. But colour is also tremendously effective in psychological terms and while the range of car colours is staggering, the manufacturers are trying to appeal to the complexity of psychological and physiological responses that colour arouses. While colour research is expanding, few customers could articulate the rationale behind choosing racing green or fiery red rather than lime green or Nevada beige. Entrances to libraries and information services are immensely important and discussed elsewhere in the text, but consider colour in this context and cover any Nevada beige as quickly as possible.

Innovation and creative approaches can enhance existing services or develop new 'offerings' or products to answer the needs of the various groups of the library's users or the information centre's clients. Academic libraries can offer very different propositions to academic staff, research students and undergraduates in their first year, in terms of access, loan opportunities, and password-protected intranet sources and activities, plus seminars for specific purposes in terms of information skilling, support for research fund seeking or faculty tuition on sources specific to the subject area. Public libraries can offer subject searching or alerting services to local businesses, specialist sessions akin to the 'clinics' of medical practices at appropriate times of the week for mothers with children, retired groups, the young unemployed, to add to the homework clubs now found in most libraries. Specialist libraries and information services will have their own subsets to cater for and packaging may be quite literal in the provision of information and materials, whether in terms of hard copy or web versions. Think of Parker: they make pens, but they are really in the gift business and successfully provide the same functional implement, in appropriate packaging, to markets ranging from schoolchildren to presidents.

Place/User convenience

Place is usually translated into 'Distribution' in a commercial marketing mix, but suits admirably for libraries and information services, since it refers to where and how a service is made available to the users and clients. That availability may be via a telecommunications network as well as or instead of a geographical location, since point of access covers a huge variety of possibilities and potential, as well as current practice, in the information world. The key word is convenience, make a service convenient to the user and service use will grow measurably. Thus a marketing mix for an educational institution, often with a main campus library plus department libraries and collections, would make a priority of a campus computer network to facilitate access to all sources.

Opening hours

Place includes accessibility, it covers 'when', as well as 'where'. The variety of opening hours and service type and availability is wide ranging. Many university libraries, for example, rely on student or auxiliary help to maintain at least an access service during the late evening or weekends. This means that even though professional user services or loan facilities are not available at all times, pressure on limited stocks and seating, and accordingly on student stress, is reduced. Loan services curtailed during such hours can have a positive effect in encouraging the user towards a more effective use of expensive, essential, but often underused periodical provision, but only if self-help user tutorials are made available or the marketing mix has included teaching sessions on the availability of various sources and the manner of their use.

Web and intranet services open up accessibility potential to a phenomenal degree, but the same caveat applies, too many resources on the web are underused or badly used. It has always been the case that user education should be paramount for the enablement of library and information service users. The problem of provision is exacerbated today by the fact that, from toddlers to silver surfers, everyone thinks that they know how to use touch-of-a-button sources and, worse, they too often accept what they see without questioning accuracy or source credibility. There is real potential here for librarians to market information skills on using the intranet, side by side with the basic courses on IT offered by the plethora of training agencies, by schools, colleges and universities. Information professionals can call it consultancy instead of training and *creating competitive intelligence at the cutting edge* instead of information skills and their clients will be delighted. Offering e-mail enquiry services needs to be matched with realistic promotion on when such services are staffed, since 24/7 access to the internet and intranet is the norm for users, and when responses can be expected.

The public library experience of branch networks should be invaluable in identifying how, when and where services may more effectively serve users. Particularly in times of reduced budgets, evaluating availability in conjunction with user need can often highlight much-needed change in terms of redistribution of services, opening hours and other methods of providing for particular publics, all the varied interested parties. Too often, branch libraries reduce opening hours in an attempt to cut costs and what results is a mish-mash of availability, so users give up. Sadly, a large UK public library authority is currently not buying fiction at all. Why? Its budgets have been reduced because of declining use. In the same authority one of its largest branches opens as follows: Monday 9–5, Tuesday 1–7, Wednesday 9–1 (except on the third Wednesday of the month when the local Member of Parliament holds his surgery for constituents), Thursday 9–7 (but this is the day of the week for late-night shopping in the town centre and the library is 20 minutes from the centre), Friday 9–5, Saturday 9–12 and 1.30–4, Sunday closed. Declining use? Or, declining to use because readers have no idea when they will find the service operating? Closing completely on Thursday and opening all day Wednesday and Saturday would go some way to restoring readers' sanity and the MP's surgeries should be monitored for attendance. These sessions could also be used as a marketing opportunity to promote information sources, since the constituents voicing concerns are also likely to be active and heard in their communities. When they are in the nursery school, doctor's surgery, pub or park, they can spread the word about the quality of the library's services.

The information centre that is providing services for an organization in, say, the industrial, medical, government or voluntary sector, needs to look at where and how it is making services available. Too often a physical base is seen to be of prime importance when, in fact, most potential users will be constrained by their situation or working practices from personal visits. Limiting service hours to those when professional information personnel are available will again hamper user potential when, as is often the case, the organization is operating on a 24-hour basis. 'We never close' may not be practicable in terms of availability of professional staff, but the situation needs to be assessed to see how online, electronic mail, auxiliary staff or user education, in say CD-ROM use, may effectively compensate. The dissemination of needed information to identified units within the organization on a regular basis is imperative and is also good public relations.

A voluntary sector unit may be able to offer only a restricted range of services, due perhaps to low funding or availability of helpers. It is essential that the limited service is managed to allow for maximum effectiveness. The type of help on offer, and where and when it is available, needs to be fully explained to potential users. A consistent pattern of service availability, even though restricted, is better than attempting to operate a service on an 'as often as possible' basis. Telephone-answering machines, even decent-sized and prominent letter-boxes, will reduce users' frustrations, especially if it is made absolutely clear when the service will be in full operation. A frequently asked questions facility, available by website or answering machine can also aid in user satisfaction.

It is tempting to make all available staff time user-access time, but it is much more effective to ensure that professional staff have dedicated time for preparation, training and in-depth enquiry work. It is usual now to see notices in large retail stores and also in some public libraries, advising that training is carried out at certain times, usually early weekday mornings, and that service starts later on that day. Small information centres that are an integral part of a larger organization might find it physically difficult to close off user access, but a determination to provide such time will pay off. Telephone calls can be diverted and even in open-plan environments screens can be used effectively. It is vital that messages or requests left during such times are answered rapidly when full service resumes, providing a good-quality service that will aid the continuing campaign for more support and resources.

Mobile services

Rural areas and the housebound are well used to mobile services. There have been some exciting ventures too in promotional activities in the use of specially converted buses, as well as the more usual library van. It is worth considering experimenting with regular mobile services to situations within the community where there are large groups of people who are disadvantaged by not having easy access to library services. Better again if such services could include the extra added value of reference services via computer links and a rapid delivery service of materials or information not carried. Poetry collections are delivered and enjoyed alongside the postal deliveries in the High-lands of Scotland. Collections could be tailored to the needs of many special groups. A new housing estate will have a preponderance of young mothers needing materials for their offspring, certainly, but their personal needs will be much wider. A sheltered housing complex will often be in a well-developed community and yet the residents will welcome a regular doorstep service since they are not fit enough to visit local amenities easily. The public relations value of these services is inestimable, whether for the elderly, infirm, isolated villages or busy urban hinterland, especially when very often this is the segment of the community who are articulate, who have the time and who have the vote.

The traditional industrial estates and the new high-technology parks are also obvious targets for mobile services. These are concentrated populations, often served by banks, post offices and sandwich shops, but rarely considered by libraries. The nature of such industrial estates and parks is that they are on the outer fringes of urban development and thus working hours tend to be extended for employees because of travelling difficulties. Equally, as lunch breaks tend to be short since there is nowhere to go, the unfortunate employee has little opportunity to visit branch libraries in normal opening hours. The lack of competitive facilities on such estates means that any library, public or academic, making its services available would be highly successful. Co-operation with individual companies would quickly allow for effective timetables and specific visits. This kind of activity could also generate sponsorship potential, as well as providing a platform for launching or enhancing information services for local industry and businesses. The corporate universities and learning organization culture of many organizations are crying out for potential partnerships of this kind.

Location

It is unpalatable but necessary to recognize that the user may be at risk in attempting personal visits to a service point. A public library branch in a shopping precinct that is deserted in the evening, or the university precinct, so well populated in daylight hours, can become lonely areas at night. The business information service in a tower block is surrounded by echoing corridors outside core hours of activity and the industrial information unit can be a nightmare to approach if it is within the manufacturing area of the company's business. All these represent a potential deterrent to users. Indeed, these situations are of concern to service personnel also and investigation needs to be made into methods of alleviating actual and perceived risk among staff and users alike.

Co-operation with the library or information centre authority, institution or organization will often result in better lighting or security equipment and personnel, which come out of central budgets as an added bonus. It is often the case that over time the physical environment or social or working practices will have changed gradually and it is not obvious that such factors are the cause of decreased usage. Such an example was a public library service, committed to its community, which offered a drop-in, cup-of-tea afternoon to pensioners (or third-agers as they are now) at one of its branches where use was declining alarmingly. There was no take-up of the generous offer: senior managers were not aware that the branch was virtually marooned in the midst of a network of new roads and heavy traffic flow.

Appearance and atmosphere

The physical location where a service is proffered may be, in terms of actual location, apparently unchangeable. Carnegie buildings abound across the UK. They are enormous, grand, imposing buildings and they can appear awesome. They must be changed: paintwork can do it, taking down old-fashioned partitions and opening up inner entrance doors can do it, illustrations on the windows can do it, flower displays seen from the street can help and, most of all, what will succeed is seeing people going in and out (school groups, mothers and toddlers, could you persuade the local football or cricket team to plan their tactics there?).

There are numerous, and excellent, examples of imaginative use of existing structures, as well as purpose-built public libraries and education libraries from school to university level. Private subscription libraries, often in listed buildings and expensively sited areas, have utilized marketing expertise to ensure future funding through expanded subscription lists, sponsorships and grants and the actual physical surroundings have been a hugely important element in readers' perception, and then support, of the library. Plans to change the British Library Reading Room raised an outcry across the world.

The physical attributes of place are, then, important to users, and potentially instrumental in attracting new users; they need to form a substantial part of the marketing plan.

External signposting is a good place to start and this will often be financed by the parent organization. EC funding has resulted in many city and town centres being tastefully adorned with destination signposting; co-operation with the planning department will ensure that the libraries are on appropriate signs. Equally, within an education campus or industrial complex, representations to the appropriate site maintenance departments will be all that is needed. If the information centre is in a large building, survey all possible entrances and routes to note where indications would be valid. The temptation to produce in-house computer-generated graphics should be resisted, even by the smallest of libraries or information services. Good signs, commercially designed and produced, are surprisingly inexpensive and present a quality image. Many large organizations will have a central department responsible for such activity and need only to be told what is needed.

An examination of inside physical structure should also be made with an objective eye to judge what early impressions are being made. Too many libraries do not even announce what they are, yet pride in the service will be reflected by a strong statement of identity. That identity should be clear from the initial approach: materials, typefaces and colours used will say a great deal about the services within. Discreet gold plates or foot-high red letters indicate much about the kind of service to expect. The general fabric of the building will reflect on the service offered too: well maintained, it will build confidence in the service it houses, in the same way that flaking paintwork and dingy surroundings will certainly affect perceptions adversely.

Again, co-operation with relevant departments will ensure that the maintenance programme cycle incorporates the changes that are desirable when the time comes. If the parent organization insists that a house style must be adhered to, librarians and information professionals need to ensure that their voices are heard during the planning stages if they are to escape the equivalent of bland magnolia or mock Tudor.

Given a free hand, and all buildings eventually have to be painted, and furniture replaced, it is important that careful consideration is given to what Philip Kotler calls 'atmospherics', the feeling that the organization would like to engender in users, or the image to be portrayed. It is aided or hindered by design.

A welcoming atmosphere can be created by staff well trained in customer care, the use of warm colours, comfortable seating and good use of space, plus wording of signs and notices. 'Welcome to the library' *will* welcome, whereas, 'Watch your possessions, there are thieves about' is not what you wish to see first as a reader.

Can libraries copy banks in the way that they have changed their image and public perceptions successfully? From awe-inspiring, gloomy, miserable halls of unapproachable tellers imprisoned by high barriers and grills, banks have become bright, friendly, customer-comfortable places, where tellers are at open desks, their names and smiles openly displayed. While it could be argued that some banks have gone too far with piped music forming part of the atmospherics, there is no doubt that the overall strategy of looking to the customer and providing a more comfortable atmosphere has paid dividends. Librarians can learn from other services; not every service or individual can afford to be at conferences, national or international, but simply travelling to a neighbouring authority or another university in the same region can often produce fruitful ideas.

An efficient, smoothly running organization inspires confidence in the user and this efficiency should be reflected in the way he or she is received initially by the system. Discussed further in the section on public relations in Chapter 5, initial reception must be considered here too. A library user may be fully confident in particular zones of the library's activities, but will be akin to a new user at the point of approaching a service not used before. A department store will welcome the customer with a breathing space area, unused space inside the entrance, an opportunity to decide on direction, a list of departments and guide to appropriate floors if necessary with a clear pathway to encourage the customer in. Entering most libraries or information centres the user is faced with security screens, then hives of activity, some behind desks or further screens. Quite often there are queues and no obvious pattern to proceed further; the user faces a real challenge – hardly the conducive atmospherics to communicate confidence.

Welcome your users must be the message. Wal-Mart, the American supermarket leader, employs 'greeters'. The library does not have to employ retired librarians as greeters, but it does have to examine the welcome signals to users. Do all overt and implicit signals 'say' welcome? How does a user feel walking through security screening devices, facing prohibitive notices, a myriad of blank computer screens? Users may be sophisticated in a whole variety of ways but a warm welcome will always colour their perception of the service offered.

The same rules apply to websites: welcome the user, make it easy to progress and use accessible language.

'Place', then, covers physical and virtual environment, ambience, staff and activities, as well as being the point of service offering.

Price/User cost

Price is the element of the marketing mix which for many in the library profession will be the most difficult to consider. Even where information centres are operating in a highly competitive business environment, the information professionals involved often feel uneasy with this aspect of the marketing mix. Price is, therefore, rarely used as a political or promotional tool by librarians and information professionals.

Price does not necessarily imply cash value: marketing is an exchange process and the price paid could be in terms of time, energy or other opportunity or activity forgone. Security cameras are installed, it might be said, at the expense of limiting personal freedoms. The true cost of ineffective user education leading to poor information-seeking skills could be inestimable when medical research is not identified in time, orders are lost in a competitive field because of poor intelligence gathering or young people make life-planning decisions on inadequate information. The price to be paid by a community might be a decision to resource other leisure activities rather than better library facilities.

The standard economic equation and calculations to achieve returns on investments, as used by other organizations, are only part of the strategic decision-making process for library and information professionals. Libraries have operated for centuries on a co-operative basis and the debates on public library charging issues will continue well into this century. In the meantime, income generation is a fact of life.

In some sectors, a new, highly coveted service might command a premium charge, as would very personalized information services for individual or specific purposes. Immediately problems arise, of where, and to whom, such services would be offered; who might be disadvantaged by not having the services available to them? As the demand for a service continues and perhaps increases, do prices stay at the same level, reduce or increase? Should public libraries charge business users on the basis of time taken over reference enquiries? Would a delivery service of information or materials produce viable revenue? When considering pricing there are a number of marketing practices that are on the face of it more relevant to commercial sectors, but that may well be applied elsewhere in concept.

Costs could differ according to *demand levels*, for example a university undergraduate who needs a tutor's or faculty librarian's signature on an interlibrary loan request will seriously consider the need for that request when weighed against the bother involved.

Market skimming aims a new product or service at a relatively small proportion of a market and charges a high price. A new database or highly selective, specialized information provision in terms of subject content or speed of provision might be introduced. If this strategy is chosen, it is particularly important that the product or service must be of excellent quality and be very different from what is otherwise available. Market skimming is not a long-term strategy: a good product or service will soon be copied by other information suppliers. The original library or information provider can benefit further by introducing cheaper or modified versions to a larger market and ahead of competition.

Market penetration in pricing terms is the opposite of skimming: a new product or service will aim at building a large user base quickly by offering the product at a low price. Economies of scale operate and, in addition, market penetration builds customer habit so that competition has difficulty in becoming established. Photocopying, video rental and even refreshment services can produce such benefits in most libraries. Offering internet access cheaply, or free, is a successful ploy in the public library sector as are information bulletins with reliable sector information in commercial information services.

Price discrimination strategies are practised widely. Special groups such as children, students, old-age pensioners and the unemployed are often offered reduced prices, and libraries could reduce standard charges for them; the increase in the use of these services would more than make up any shortfall caused by the reduction. Services or products are often reduced according to the time of day, or year, in which they are used or bought: rail travel off-peak, pizza and pub happy hours, central heating installed in summer, Monday night theatre seats are just a few examples. Extra loans could be allowed during lower-use days and it could perhaps be made conditional that they must be returned in a corresponding period.

Family subscriptions to a private library at an advantageous rate will happily mean a likelihood that the children will continue membership as they reach adulthood.

Pricing always needs to be examined carefully. Charging by volume of use is a minefield. A university library may well charge a higher subscription rate to a professional society or body with a large membership list, and a very much smaller rate to a relatively smaller body; yet it could well be that the volume and type of use made by the membership of the smaller society is very much more demanding.

A business might be prepared to pay an external provider for information that adds substantially to competitive intelligence, but might be unhappy about putting a price on its own in-house provision of services especially as the use of extranets grows. Discussing these problems at senior management level will highlight the value of the company's information service whatever the eventual decision.

And finally, yet another factor before deciding on pricing strategy: price often implies value in the mind of the user and is taken to be an index of quality. Parents will often buy materials to support their children's development or education, when the library could provide much better resources freely. The marketing mix needs to stress other benefits of the service to overcome this type of market behaviour.

Promotion/User communication

Librarians and information professionals are confident here, because they have had more practice in this area of marketing than any other. Marketing communication is a better description than is 'promotion' of the activities involved – and the one, incidentally, preferred by Kotler. Librarians and information professionals will confidently claim that their communication skills are good; marketing expertise will channel and focus those skills to even greater effect.

It is helpful to consider the aspects of a marketing communications mix or promotions mix as a subset of the marketing mix and as a highly integrated part of that mix. Where libraries and information services have not been happy with the results of, often heavily resourced, promotional efforts, it has usually been where the promotional programme has been planned in isolation. It is important to remember, too, that even comparatively simple promotion activity has a real cost in staff energy and time, to which must be added either the loss of the work with which staff would otherwise have been involved or the cost of other staff doing that work. The mantra for all librarians and information professionals hardly needs repeating – *communication is a two-way process*.

Promotion, publicity and public relations methods are discussed in greater detail in Chapter 5.

Planning the communications mix

A return to the mission of the library and information service and firmly fixing the need for an internal as well as an external policy are vital prerequisites for drawing up objectives for the communications mix. A clear picture is needed, through recent market research where possible, of the segments to be reached, in order to decide on the most effective ways of reaching these segments. Evaluation methods must be built in at the planning stage too. Another factor for serious consideration is time, not just the appropriate timing of activities, but the need for sufficient preparation time for those involved in publicizing the activities.

Project management and critical path analysis are useful management tools to use in working with the communication mix.

Users will, of course, be continually receiving a variety of communications about the library or information service, some of which were dealt with when discussing place and price. It is vital that this is taken into account, that it forms part of the planning process and that information on user perceptions is also sought consistently.

Classic models of communication form a basis for considering fundamental factors in the planning stages: who says what, in what channel, to whom, with what effect.

A planned communications mix for a library or information service will include some or all of the following elements:

- public relations
- paid-for advertising
- publications
- salespeople.

Public relations

Public relations is defined by the UK's Institute of Public Relations as: 'the deliberate, planned and sustained effort to establish and maintain mutual understanding between an organisation and its publics'.

Who are the 'publics' of libraries and information services? Kotler (2000, 605) defines a public as: 'any group that has an actual or potential interest in or impact on a company's ability to achieve its objectives'. The library or information centre's main 'publics' with whom they need to build good relations are those listed by Wilson and Gilligan with Howsden (1995, 369): the community at large; employees; customers – past, present and future; suppliers of materials and services; the money market – the funders, shareholders, potential investors or sponsors; distributors; potential employees and opinion leaders – all those whose opinions may help or harm the organization. Local, regional and national government agencies, professional bodies and pressure groups are publics. Within the organization there are publics too, other departments or divisions, or other companies under the auspices of a parent company. An audit of communications with publics inside and outside the organization is recommended as essential. Particular attention should be paid to:

- the influence, actual and potential, of the various publics on the well-being of the library or information service
- the type, frequency and extent of communications with specific publics
- the methods of evaluating the effectiveness of communications.

It is an inescapable fact that it is impossible for the library or information service not to communicate. The elements discussed under 'Place', for example, substantially affect public relations since they are communicating a number of messages: efficient service, welcome, we care. The ways in which a telephone is answered or responses to correspondence, electronic included, are handled, affects public relations continually. Managers need to cheek for themselves, regularly, what kinds of message are being conveyed.

Paid-for advertising

Advertising channels of communication range from a small classified advertisement in the local press, through billboards and posters, radio and cinema advertisements, website plugs to prime-time television commercials. Unlikely though it may seem, even the Church of England has used television commercials, but the cost of a professional production, plus air-time, will be way beyond the budgets of many libraries and information services.

Press advertisements are not so costly, but nevertheless are a substantial call on the communications budget, and it is worth employing an advertising agency if a major campaign is planned. Advertising agencies are important in the creative processes and for making decisions on the best channels to use for reaching target markets. They can also negotiate reduced fees and test for the effectiveness of communications.

A variety of research techniques – DAGMAR (Defining Advertising Goals for Measuring Advertising Results) from Colley (1961) is one of the well known – exist to test for effectiveness, but proving that there is a relationship between advertising and any future action by the user is notoriously difficult. Lord Leverhulme is usually quoted in this context: 'half of all advertising is wasted, but the problem lies in knowing which half'.

It is important to assess where advertisements might appear most fruitfully, in terms of which media to use, and when. Auctions were once held for television commercial space in the middle of popular soap programmes and the highest bidder often came in at the very last second to upstage a rival competitor. Libraries, even large national libraries, are not going to be involved in that kind of race. However, the rapid multiplication of television channels, analogue terrestrial, satellite, cable and now digital, means that the choice of audience can be very specific according to channel and time of day, narrowcasting rather than broadcasting. This means that it may well be worth considering such advertising since the target can be very precise and the response rate probably high. Academic libraries advertising in the local community will aim at businesses as well as prospective students.

Television health programmes abound and the primary care professionals would be interested in medical collections and services. Where special collections are the subject of the advertisement, specific trade media can also be used to target professionals. Programmes for parents at mid-morning are prime advertising spots for the target audience, but not so expensive if public libraries wanted to promote new collections for parents.

Where the library or information centre pays for an advertisement (classified advertising usually), whatever the media, the actual content of the advertisement, format, place and time of appearance is under the control of the librarian or information manager. As the paying customer he or she will stipulate exactly what is required, and will pay very heavily for this benefit, depending on where in the newspaper or television schedules the advertisement is to appear. Front page, bottom right-hand corner of the newspaper is most expensive and the right-hand page on a double spread, again bottom right, is also expensive, because this is where the human eye alights first. Customers tempted by cheap rates in the gutter margin are wasting their money. It is firmly recommended that libraries use a press release rather than advertising for events and public announcements. (How to put together an effective press release is discussed in Chapter 5.)

Publications

Publications are discussed elsewhere as products; for example from the business information centre come business reports, specialist monographs, training manuals, statistical surveys; from the public library there are collections of photographs or calendars from local history collections, anthologies of creative writing, book reviews or poetry; from the academic sector there are subject bibliographies and texts on how to cite and reference, and abstracting and indexing services abound. The majority of such publications will be in paper and electronic format. It is not always the best policy to insist on a house style for all publications, but what is essential is to ensure that the library or information service is clearly portrayed as the originator, creator or publisher of the publication. The role of publications manager, or more likely set of responsibilities in a smaller information centre, might be one that is conducive to the talents and skills of a specific member of staff. The existence of such a post, or responsible colleague, would encourage staff who are specialists in particular areas, but wary of the whole publication process, to participate in the publications programme as part of marketing activity. Utilizing talents of a variety of kinds in this way motivates staff, leads to a higher profile and more effective products.

The 'sales force'

One of the *Concise Oxford dictionary* definitions of selling, is 'to advertise, or publish merits of; give information on value of something; inspire with desire to buy or acquire or agree to something'.

A business organization in the information industry will deploy a sales force in the field, dedicated to selling the important products of the company. It is not envisaged that the libraries and information services which are the market for this text would be employing sales personnel to any extent. It is suggested, however, that all employees be encouraged to recognize their very real role as salespeople for the organization. Their role will be to make customer care a high-level priority, presenting a professional face at all times to establish and develop good public relations. In a restaurant, the food, environment and price may be right, but a customer will only come back as a regular client if the service is good and he or she is made to feel comfortable and a welcome visitor. Kotler (1999, 9) argues that 'meeting customer expectations will only *satisfy* customers: exceeding their expectations will *delight* them'.

All employees must be convinced of their own worth and value to the library or information service so that they become effective members of the sales force. Training and development in the personal areas of self-worth and confidence are as important as job knowledge and skills provision. Staff who are confident in the importance of their own role in caring for clients will be an effective force in building up good public relations. Telephonists, receptionists, porters, couriers, all have their role to play in this culture. So too do the specialist personnel who may need even more convincing that they have a public relations role as well as a professional one.

It is interesting to note that in training sales personnel, there are generally recognized to be two basic approaches: one where high-pressure selling techniques are emphasized and achievement targets are set, the volume of sales being absolute priority; the other, which is much more customer oriented, where the concentration is on analysing and answering customer needs and the consequent benefits to the customer, leading to confidence and loyalty on the part of the customer. The marketing approach of the latter is much more palatable to the librarian or information professional who may still feel that the concept of selling is distasteful.

Another aspect of the communications mix is to identify influential committees or groups and ensure that library or information personnel are nominated and selected as members. The more integrated a department becomes, the more readily the rest of the organization accepts its importance. The effectiveness is doubled when the library or information centre invites others to participate in its own activities.

Membership of internal committees is valuable and effective public relations. Equally so is the active participation of library and information personnel on relevant, and preferably influential, external groups. The strategy should be to identify key areas where a presence would be valuable and to select staff who will make a real contribution, both in the work of the group and in bringing back knowledge and expertise to share with colleagues.

Communication is the vital ingredient

Communication within the organization is a vital component of marketing philosophy and for some information services, particularly within some government sectors, might even be a priority over external communications. The way in which everyday routine activities are tackled, including staff communication, reflects the philosophy of an organization. In the library or information service that respects and truly cares about users this philosophy will permeate all its activities.

Resources

A major difficulty for most libraries is that they will not have an easily identified promotions budget, or that the parent authority or organization will see promotional effort as being a whole-organization policy. Identifying key personnel and committees and appropriate lobbying then become part of the communications mix. Where information units have the same problem, but external communications are very much part of the centre's work, a substantial case for extra funding will need to be made. A good communications mix needs a clearly apportioned resource bank, personnel included, and a good set of evaluative procedures that will provide the needed evidence of the value of a well-resourced programme.

A planned marketing mix is expensive; the costs may be heavily disguised in training budgets, publications budgets, postal costs, staff salaries and the like, but it is wise management strategy to quantify real costs in order to make a persuasive case for more resources. If a public relations consultancy is called in for a specific purpose or campaign, real costs are then inescapable. The control of the marketing policy is a senior management function and, given the sustained effort involved, it should be recognized as a substantial workload and appropriate support given to internal staff, even where an external public relations consultancy is employed.

The marketing mix aims at communicating effectively with the 'publics' of the library or information service and satisfying target user, client and customer needs. It is a significant and substantial part of marketing policy that supports the mission and corporate image of the library or information service. Marketing policy must have serious resources to underpin it. Its success could mean the difference between merely surviving and real growth and development, and this success is very largely based on understanding market need.

References and further reading

Borden, N. H. (1965) The concept of the marketing mix. In Schwartz, G. (ed.) *Science in marketing*, Wiley, 386–97.

Brassington, F. and Pettit, S. (2000) *Principles of marketing*, Pitman.

Christopher, M. and McDonald, M. (1995) *Marketing: an introductory text*, Macmillan.

Colley, R. H. (1961) *Defining advertising goals for measured advertising results*, Association of National Advertisers.

Jefkins, F. (2000) *Advertising*, 4th edn, revised and edited by Daniel Yadin, Pearson Education.

Kotler, P. (1973–4) Atmospherics as a marketing tool, *Journal of Retailing*, (Winter), 48–64.

Kotler, P. (1984) *Marketing management*, 5th edn, Prentice Hall.

Kotler, P. (1999) *Kotler on marketing*, The Free Press.

Kotler, P. (2000) *Marketing management: the millennium edition*, 10th edn, Prentice Hall.

Lauterborn, R. (1990) New marketing litany: 4P's passé; C-words take over, *Advertising Age*, (1 October), 26.

McCarthy, E. J. (1978) *Basic marketing: a managerial approach*, 6th edn, Irwin.

Mazur, L. (1991–2) Silent satisfaction, *Marketing Business*, (December–January), 24–7.

Meldrum, M. and McDonald, M. (1995) *Key marketing concepts*, Macmillan.

Wilson, R. M. S. and Gilligan, C. with Howsden, M. (1995) *Strategic marketing management*, Butterworth-Heinemann.

Zeithaml, V. A. and Bitner, M. J. (2000) *Services marketing: integrating customer focus across the firm*, McGraw-Hill.

5

PROMOTION AND PUBLIC RELATIONS

There are any number of ways to communicate with target audiences: via media – print, broadcast and internet – direct mail, at the point of contact with the organization and even in the use of effective packaging. Librarians and information professionals must integrate the various methods into a cohesive programme that is planned, resourced and evaluated as part of the strategic marketing plan.

The objectives of this chapter are:

- to explore further types of promotion in the marketing mix
- to define public relations
- to identify the publics of the library and information centre who are targets for promotion and public relations activities.

It is *impossible* not to communicate – this cannot be stressed too strongly to senior management and staff. The communication method that libraries and information centres will use as the major tool in their promotional mix will almost certainly be public relations. Public relations is defined by the UK's Institute of Public Relations as: *'The deliberate, planned and sustained effort to establish and maintain mutual understanding between an organisation and its publics'*. A vibrant, positive image will not be promoted by poor physical maintenance and disillusioned staff, but with committed staff even a small service can use a good public relations strategy to effect.

The 'poor image' of libraries, and by implication information centres, is largely in the minds of the librarians and professionals themselves; the larger publics tend to be, on the whole, completely indifferent. Changing that indifference to positive approbation is the work of public relations.

Planned public relations, continuous and consistent, can be far more influential than advertising, which will tend to be used rarely, for major events only if at all, and will be expensive. Librarians and information professionals must recognize that a public relations policy, its planning and its implementation, carry substantial human resource implications, of which senior management must be persuaded also.

Public relations planning

Librarians and information professionals must aim at stimulating the target market's interest, inculcating an understanding of what the library and information centre is about and what it has to offer and encouraging use of the service.

As part of the planning process they need to ask:

- Who are the target audiences?
- What kind of action or behaviour is wanted from the target audience?
- What are the messages to be communicated?
- What kinds of channels will be effective in reaching the target audience?
- What resources are needed?

Publics

Wilson and Gilligan with Howsden (1995, 367) maintain that public relations is, at its simplest, the way in which an organization manages its relations with its publics.

Who are the 'publics', the target audiences for public relations strategy, of libraries and information centres? As we saw in Chapter 4, public is any group or body that has an actual or potential interest in, or impact on, the ability of the library or information centre to achieve its objectives. Publics might include all or many of the following:

- parent organizations or authorities
- financial backers
- government (local, national and sometimes international)
- politically influential bodies
- the media
- professional associations
- social groups
- employees
- trades unions
- suppliers
- users and clients.

What must be realized is that Wilson's 'simple' does not equate with 'easy': public relations is a continual process involving every aspect of the organization and all members of staff at every level. A public relations policy should continually seek to satisfy clients' and users' needs for excellent quality of service and to focus staff energies on maintaining standards at a high level in users' perceptions. Where a strong, positive attitude towards the library or information centre is developed, the users are less likely to change their habits. The whole purpose of a public relations strategy is to engender that positive feeling in all of the groups related to or affecting the library or information centre.

The employment of public relations professionals is now commonplace both in the commercial and public world, and to support 'celebrities' in politics, sport and entertainment. In the UK, the Queen, the Church of England and Oxford University all employ public relations staff to manage their public affairs. They deal with image management, issues management and crisis management. There are libraries and information centres that employ marketing managers who include public relations in their job description, but on the whole most services will need to designate a member, or members, of their current staff to manage public relations.

Creating awareness

Significant sectors of the potential market for the library or information centre's services are probably not aware of all the services available or have no understanding at all of what is on offer. This can be a real opportunity to create new relationships and enhance existing users' perceptions. The media will use information about libraries and information centres as 'news'. Visitors will come to an exhibition in library premises as happily as to one mounted in a gallery, museum, shopping mall or purpose-built visitors' attraction of the 21st century. Corporate sponsors with massive community budgets will be interested in generating positive attitudes in cause-related marketing with library partners in the public and education sector. Corporate magazines will be happy to carry regular articles from the company's information officer when slanted to reflect current issues.

Every opportunity needs to be taken to build awareness of the library and information centre. Every appropriate agenda must include the library or information centre; signposts are needed everywhere; press releases for print and broadcast media must be produced as the norm; regular items must appear in student magazines; in-house journals and bulletins must have regular columns; internet websites must carry a 'news' page; intranet and extranet websites need contributions regularly; open days can encourage different market groups to 'see behind the scenes'; exhibitions, displays and talks are all good possibilities; greetings cards listing public library services can be sent to all new members of the community (via estate agents and local councils or churches); a personal introduction to services for all new company personnel – the list is endless.

The public relations plan might include all or some of these and more. They all aim at attracting attention and creating a positive attitude in the target market. They aim at presenting a message: a message that the target market will pay attention to, comprehend, retain and be influenced by in their behaviour. The target market may also influence other markets: an academic library will want lecturers to stress the value of information skills to their students and reward submitted academic work displaying good bibliographies; a public library will want parents to promote a visit to the library to their children, as an enjoyable educational or recreational activity; a company information centre will want section heads to pass on to their team the value of the centre's resources for staff development.

A corporate information centre has a particular need to identify influential groups. 'Special libraries can disappear from the corporate landscape if they don't make themselves an integral part of the organization's operations . . . there isn't a large community to rally to their aid' (Wolfe, 1997, 182). Information professionals in the commercial sector were told to 'move on' if they could not persuade their management teams of the competitive value of information, at the 11th European Business Information Conference (Harrington, 2001) by the president of the Thomson Corporation. No library or information centre can leave public relations out of their strategic planning.

AIDA: a communication model

The librarian and information professional will have particular objectives for specific promotional or public relations activities, as well as general overall objectives with regard to building and maintaining the perception of a highly regarded quality organization and service. The response sought from the user or client will usually fall into one of three categories: cognitive, affective or behavioural. Thus the communication mix for a promotion or for public relations should aim at making the user aware, or at changing user perceptions, or actually encouraging the user to do something.

A number of response-hierarchy models exist, but one of the most attractive and effective to use, as well as the most widely known marketing model, is AIDA:

- **A**wareness – awareness is triggered, among users and potential users, of the library or information centre and services offered.
- **I**nterest – interest is stimulated in users and potential users in what is on offer and why.
- **D**esire – users want to find out more and potential users are attracted to the idea of using the service.

- **A**ction – the target markets use the service or feel positive towards the service.

The time taken to move each target segment of users or potential users through the various stages will differ according to the objectives of the marketing plan. A communication mix may, for example, aim at achieving the cognitive or affective stages fairly quickly initially, arriving gradually thereafter at the behaviour stage. A more direct approach would aim at arriving at the action stage very rapidly. The desired timespan needs careful planning; encouraging action at too early a stage can be disastrous. Creating demand before the information service is readily available, or before there are sufficient materials to meet users' requirements or personnel to staff the service, leads to frustration and rebounds badly on the library or information centre. Launching a website without adequate back-up maintenance and sufficient staff for a quick response service is all too common. The resulting long-term loss of prestige is much more difficult to manage than the promotion of the new initiative.

Awareness – the cognitive stage

The first step in the communication process is to attract attention: the telephone rings, bleeps, flashes a light or plays a favourite jingle, the ambulance siren blares. It is sad and obvious, but needs repeating, that libraries for too long relied on the knowledge that they were offering a valuable service and expected potential users to know that. Academic libraries have captive markets to a great extent, but again will often expect users to know that special collections or specific services exist. Academic teaching staff will be highly expert and well versed in the facilities supporting their own specialities, but may not be aware of what else is available from which their students as well as they themselves could benefit. In the business and industrial sector, personnel may have a skewed perception of what the company's information service is about, if indeed they know that the company has a service at all. Professional bodies will often offer a range of information services to members, but too often there is nothing other than a short paragraph in a membership introduction pack to draw attention to them.

The message is, librarians and information professionals must draw attention to services without being shocking, offensive, or causing traffic accidents. Benetton clothing advertisements shocked the world with graphic scenes of death in war and childbirth; fcuk, another clothing fashion chain, used the anagram of the company name, French Connection UK, to attract attention; Wonderbra billboard advertisements, at heavy traffic flow areas, were condemned. For professional services it is not true that bad publicity is better than no publicity: libraries and information services should be 'squeaky clean' institutions if they are to retain credibility and impress their target markets.

Interest and Desire – the affective stage

Selected market segments must be researched and analysed to identify what characteristics of a communication will trigger interest. The benefits to the selected segment need to be highlighted; careful use of illustrations, situations and people will aid self-recognition and move the audience on to the next stage, desire to obtain the benefits. Segmentation is discussed in depth in Chapter 6, but a useful exercise for librarians and information professionals is to examine the successful range of publications, television advertisements and websites that have been produced to attract users to banking services. The same banking services essentially are on offer to all, loans and savings, money management, but a range of communications are fronted with illustrations that depict schoolchildren, young professionals, students, young marrieds, families and the senior generation, and use language appropriate to these market segments. The receiver identifies with the appearance and lifestyle of those portrayed and the message is clear – these services are for you.

Action – the behaviour stage

The inducements to action in the consumer-goods sector are myriad: coupons offering price reductions; two for the price of one, or buy two and the third is free; premium offers which give more for the same price or a gift attached to the purchase; banded packs of linked items e.g. coffee and biscuits; free samples or demonstrations. Can librarians and information professionals follow suit?

An invitation addressed personally can be a powerful inducement to a potential user; staff need to be on hand at the stated times and preferably identified in the invitation. Exhibitions, especially if staffed at appropriate times, can be as effective as in-store demonstrations; such apparently unlikely organizations as the Inland Revenue and the Law Society operate successful exhibitions in public thoroughfares. All shopping centres have weeks of the year when their 'footfall' figures, shoppers passing by, are low. They depend on community-type activities at these times to enliven their shopping malls. Public and education sector libraries could mount professional exhibitions, perhaps with IT resources, especially interactive, to attract attention to their services and resources at times when shoppers have time and space to participate. Costs are likely to be negligible in comparison with the resulting exposure and rise in service use as people act on the personal approach or advice.

Premium offers might be free time on a new online service if using an existing service; Dialog is among many service providers to use this method successfully and that type of 'offer' might be negotiated for library and information centre users as well as professional staff.

The availability of new technology might be an initial attraction, but if backed by the promise of specialized personnel and individual attention via an appointment system it is much more likely to produce user action.

To their credit, public librarians in the UK have initiated visits to organizations such as working men's clubs and women's institutes to draw attention to their services. They distributed materials on loan and were highly gratified as the books came back into the branches and registration forms were filled in for these new users. Librarians in other countries have been equally enterprising. Such activities, sadly, tend to be sporadic and dependent on individual staff or groups of personnel. Information professionals in the commercial and industrial sectors tend not to do this sort of thing, but could go into the social workspace, dining areas and sports facilities of their companies to promote their services with panache.

Professional co-operation and promotion

With the ease of communication via the internet and e-mail, professional associations and organizations could co-operate more in raising the generic profile of libraries and information services. Professional textbooks and journals, conferences and workshops play an invaluable part in the sharing of knowledge, but there must be a mass of excellent grass-root activity which could well benefit the whole community of professional practice were it to be shared more readily.

Professionals are not normally in competition with other library or information centres and their co-ordinated strength has the potential to be a tremendous marketing force. Where groups are meeting for professional purposes, including virtually, it would be a step forward were marketing to be introduced to their agenda as a priority.

There is a need for an open sharing of failures as well as successes to aid the learning processes. Also, physical artefacts might be shared and travelling exhibitions and displays mounted, sponsorship contacts and opportunities could be transferred or exchanged, media 'stories' could be rewritten for use in other authorities or states, bibliographic, abstracting and indexing services might be prepared co-operatively but with individual service logos on publications.

The media

Relationships

The enormous amount of newspaper and journal space, and radio and television air-time, both terrestrial and digital, that needs to be filled means that a good relationship with the various forms of media will always produce results in making publics aware of the library or information service.

Producing good press releases to distribute to the media is a communication skill, but it does not demand the skills of the advertising copywriter or jour-nalist. Librarians and information professionals can quickly become adept in producing effective releases. The techniques to consider are discussed at the end of the chapter, since almost all of the examples discussed could be the subject of a press release or sometimes a press conference.

Stories for the press

There is real scope for co-operation among the profession in story cultiva-tion. The business pages of the *Sunday Times* contained a full-page spread of articles on the Patent Office, complete with quotes and 'stories'. One story, for example, concerned a company that had wasted valuable time and money on product research before searching for solutions in existing patents, only to realize, to their embarrassment, that their own company had patented the solution – 30 years before. The articles covered the role of the British Library, Patents Online and Patent Express and the British Library website. They also mentioned the 13 Patent Information Network libraries spread across the regions of the UK, each and every one of which could have contacted their local media to develop the 'local gloss', with their own stories and details of contacts who are users of the service. Patent libraries in other countries could use the *Sunday Times* example as a template for their own business press.

In larger libraries or information centres, it is vital to identify one person to whom interesting events or stories can be channelled for onward trans-mission to the appropriate media – a press officer. The 'press officer' needs the support of senior management in encouraging a marketing culture throughout the library or information centre, so that every member of staff regards it as part of their own responsibility to supply information.

Exciting, innovative items are not going to be in the library's calendar every week, but anything that has a local slant will be of interest and apparently mun-dane items about long service awards, for example, will be published.

In an organization that has an in-house journal or newsletter, the infor-mation centre should seek to be mentioned in at least every other issue, and preferably have a regular column.

New personnel will be a continuing source of potential material, but naturally their permission is needed before their personal details are released, internally or externally. It is highly unlikely that the community will take in that the new librarian or information officer has two Siamese cats and an interest in Japanese art, but the impression of an organization that is attracting new blood and moreover is a people-oriented organization will have been quietly emphasized.

Local media

The general ignorance of what today's libraries and information services are about does give enormous scope for a whole bank of items to which attention might be drawn. Library and information services are people-oriented businesses, success is virtually assured. As well as reaching potential users, local media continuously and vigorously reach the people who are influential or are the decision makers when it comes to resourcing the community's libraries.

To prove that it is worth doing and provide ideas to copy in the future, a short period of scanning the local press, including the free sheets and radio and television news bulletins, will identify the organizations feeding the media successfully.

Radio

Radio, particularly community radio, is beginning to emerge as a strong contender in the promotion arena. Twenty-four hours a day, seven days a week multiplied by the number of radio broadcasting channels and programmes is a powerful promotional tool. Educational institutions in particular are using this medium successfully. Selecting the programmes that are reaching target audiences is comparatively easy; communicating a clear message, while that audience is usually involved in other activities as well as listening to the radio, is not so easy, but the listener's imagination is an ally in constructing powerful images. Libraries might like to consider proposing contributions for regular slots about materials and services for children, the business community or students, as well as offering to support, for example, gardening programmes with comment on new publications.

Web articles

Web articles are often acceptable from external contributors. Trade sites, e-zines and newsletters of specialist groups are all prime targets for such articles. Synergy with the library or information centre's user base must be considered and making contact with the site owners for editorial advice is advisable before submission. It is important to be topical and internet users are fascinated by information about the internet and its users, so articles about statistical surveys of user behaviour, searching techniques and useful information sources will be readily accepted. Specialist staff in the library, say the children's librarian or the local history specialist (both areas are huge markets for internet users), can be encouraged to produce information that can be written up by a designated member of staff if they have neither the time nor inclination to do so themselves. Information centre staff who are familiar with writing reports as part of their daily routine will be more confident in writing such articles but may need equal encouragement.

Media ratings

Paid-for advertising will not be in the plan or budget for most libraries and information centres. Nevertheless librarians and information professionals will benefit from a knowledge of which titles, newspaper and journal, and broadcasting media are reaching which market segments, to aid in drawing up mailing lists for press releases and deciding where to put best efforts in contacting which media.

The UK media bible, which provides information on specific space and timings cost, is *British Rate and Data*, known as BRAD; it appears monthly. Information on UK readership and audiences is readily available: the National Readership Survey from NRS Ltd samples 30,000 readers annually; BARB, the Broadcasters' Audience Research Board, continues to use the systems of JICTAR (Joint Industry Committee for Television Advertising Research) to measure TV programme audiences from a national sample of homes with specially metered sets; JICRAR (Joint Industry Committee for Radio Advertising Research) surveys radio listeners and is produced by Radio Joint Audience Research (RAJAR), jointly owned by BBC Radio and AIRC, the UK commercial radio association); and JICPAS, later JICPAR (Joint Industry Committee for Poster Advertising Research) provides information on posters. An excellent guide to these and other European and international organizations in media research is provided by Chisnall's (2001) *Marketing research*, now in its 6th edition. All of these surveys are well established and, whilst they do have their critics and new methods are under consideration, they still offer a substantial yardstick for media planners. Nielsen Media Research, a reputable well-established ratings measurement company, measures web and banner traffic with Netratings by tracking internet users.

Public Service Announcements

Public Service Announcements (PSAs) are short promotional films on community services produced by local commercial television networks. They have had a reputation in the past for being dire in presentation: old-fashioned formats, laughable voiceovers and put out at times when the audience would be minimal, i.e. in the slots that companies would not pay for. The focus on providing a service for the community – in the UK this is a requisite for TV companies obtaining a franchise – has changed all that. Professional help is available in producing the most appropriate form of message and the resulting product is given reasonable slots in the schedules. All of this is free, but it does take up substantial time in preparation and would be available only for specific services meeting a TV company's criteria of a community service.

Tom Cannon (1996, 350–2) regrets that the rigour of defining advertising goals is 'often neglected in favour of detailed discussion of specific creative presentation'. Cannon's advertising goals are:

- to inform specific target groups within a specified timescale
- to build an image or highlight certain features
- to reinforce specific behaviour patterns.

There is good sense in this, whether discussing a Public Service Announcement or an advertising campaign with an external agency, internal public relations department or library and information centre staff. The focus has to be the intended audience and the message. It is very easy for costs to spiral, even for a PSA, and creative, artistic and aesthetic forces to cloud the message. We all remember specific beautiful, evocative television advertisements but often retain no clue in that memory of the product message.

E-public relations

The keywords for electronic public relations are 'reputation, relevance and relations' (Haig, 2000, 10).

The inauguration and maintenance of an attractive website is mandatory for any organization's public relations strategy in the 21st century. A trawl of existing websites will quickly identify strengths to be sought and weaknesses to be avoided. Sites that contain news sections but that are not updated continually are harmful to any organization's image, even more so to a library or information centre, whose lifeblood is information and its presentation. The detrimental effect of out-of-date websites in public relations terms can be catastrophic.

Janal (2000, 14) advises being creative in using links: users will always leave the site, so make it pleasant for them, give them useful links, to associations, news sources, and they will return. The more successful sites build relationships with their target markets through interactivity, both interactivity with the library or information centre site and interactivity facilitated between users, such as chat facilities and bulletin boards. Haig (2000, 40) says give users something to click on to satisfy 'itchy-finger syndrome, an over-bearing desire to click on a mouse at least once every fifteen seconds'.

Treating the internet as another media channel was discussed earlier in this chapter under 'Web articles' (p. 90). E-mail marketing is included later in this chapter under 'Direct marketing'. Internet, extranet and intranet presence are discussed more fully in Chapter 7 'Marketing in the digital age'.

Sponsorship

This is usually considered in the context of who might be approached for funding, and is now a major business. Companies exist to match organizations looking for sponsorship opportunities with those who are seeking sponsors. Fund-granting foundations and organizations are legion; they employ professional staff who are happy to support potential applicants in the early stages of preparing bids. Business in the local community will, in most cases, be more likely to respond to requests than the large global organizations, which are deluged with applications. The benefits of the sponsorship to those approached need to be made crystal clear and access to a desired segment of the market is often a winning ploy.

Sponsorship for a library or information service can take many forms, for example supporting one-off events such as exhibitions, funding important purchases, providing resources for a working writer or artist in residence, producing a video or specialist publication, or subsidizing a building programme. A specialist collection or reading room might be given a name incorporating the sponsor in return for funding. Happily this confers a moral obligation on the sponsor to ensure the future upkeep of the facility bearing the sponsor's name in order to preserve their own good image.

Any request for sponsorship should state specifically why commitment is sought and what type of support is needed; supporting evidence may be attached, but the initial letter should be short, professional and to the point. Librarians and information professionals seeking sponsorship must remember that it is important to pay attention to how results of the activities to be funded will be disseminated.

Sponsorship can be in kind and not just financial. Technology, hardware and software, might be donated or specialist staff 'loaned' to the library or information centre. Warehousing or storage facilities are expensive and could be offered by companies who are reducing capacity.

There is still a sense of wariness about sponsorship, almost a distaste for sponsorship activity, although there are some excellent sponsorship initiatives in the library and information world. The British Library galleries, for example, have benefited in digitization activity with commercial partners and the library suppliers in particular recognize the reciprocity of sponsorship. Peter Brooke, UK Secretary of State for National Heritage in 1992, was 'concerned to encourage the expansion of total resources for libraries by developing sponsorship from the private sector. Even a small amount of external income can have a disproportionately beneficial effect upon the library service' (Aslib, 1992, Foreword).

Who to approach

Reflected glory works both ways in corporate identity terms, so potential partnerships or sponsorship arrangements need to be considered carefully. A good example of how two top calibre organizations can mutually benefit and be enhanced by the partner's reputation is the arrangement between the British Library and Digital Equipment Company. Digital provides the British Library with computer systems integral to automated user-services and in return an innovative, interactive exhibition gallery in the British Library bears Digital's name.

Before approaching companies it would be wise to assess whether their product or service range is truly complementary to the library or information service mission and activities. A company that desires to show itself as being socially responsible may be trying to cloak the effects of some of its activities, which could rebound badly on the library or service.

Sponsorship is a business transaction between two equal partners, both of whom are investing in the relationship. As with any good relationship, it follows that communication between the parties is essential and to be nurtured. The sponsor will be seeking benefits and access to markets that match the company's objectives. The library or information centre will have eliminated companies or organizations that do not match their own aims and objectives at an early stage, but it is still important to establish an understanding of both partners' motives and aims, through dialogue and negotiation, as early as possible. This is even more important if a number of partners are involved so that a good return on the investment can be made.

Being a sponsor

The library or information centre itself can be a sponsor. Sponsorship does not have to be in the form of the library or information centre offering finance: it could be perhaps premises offered free of charge, or support for publications through printing or distribution. It may be possible to consider joint sponsorship ventures with a partner providing most of the finance and the library or information service providing displays, materials or manpower.

The types of event or activity sponsored should complement the desired image of the library or information service; most kinds of topical information programmes, 'awareness weeks', or a youth-theatre production or vigorous local charity work would be examples where public relations might well be enhanced.

Exhibitions

Participating as an exhibitor

Exhibitions, not to be confused with displays, need to be assessed on their potential for communicating with target markets, against the cost of participation. There are many types of exhibition where libraries and information units would benefit from having a presence: industrial and trade exhibitions, agricultural shows, education fairs at home and abroad. The nature of the exhibition, who will be attracted and in what numbers, and who else will be exhibiting, will affect decisions on whether to participate.

Professional participation includes the cost of a stand, materials for display and professional staff to be present. Participation should only be considered if it is going to be professional; anything less will be to the detriment of the public image aimed for. Costs can be cut, especially if the exhibition is abroad, by joining forces with other organizations and enlisting the support of government departments for trade and industry.

Many universities are seeking to make their presence felt on the international scene, for purposes of sponsorship as well as student enrolment, and the rating of their information services departments can make a crucial difference when university ambassadors are abroad. Information centres in business and industry should be facets of the organization or company's activities that are worthy of highlighting anywhere that the organization or company is exhibiting. This will not necessarily bring the information centre more users, but it will cement its existence and value firmly in the minds of the chairman, influential board members and directors who see it there. Publications of the information centre will play a good public relations role in the exhibition environment too.

Hosting exhibitions

It is valuable to consider using the premises of the library or information centre to host exhibitions for other organizations or groups. This is done particularly successfully when university and public libraries have space and, equally importantly, staff in dedicated public relations, design or exhibition-officer posts. Libraries not in this fortunate position could consider seeking sponsorship and borrow such staff on short-term contract as an alternative to buying in external agencies. If the latter is considered, it is best to choose a public relations company that specializes in such work: some see exhibition work as a fringe activity.

The pay-off is in the visitors to the exhibition, who will now be very much aware of the library's existence and who may well be attracted to services offered. In addition, all the surrounding publicity that the exhibition has generated will benefit the service.

The information centre, however large, will rarely be in a position to invite large numbers through its doors to participate in exhibitions, confidentiality of work being a restraining factor.

Displays

These will provide the information centre with a shop window and could be positioned in the foyer of the company or organization, or in the refectory, board-room or on the shop floor, depending on the market segments aimed at and the centre's objectives. Professional presentation, good timing and dismantling on time are ingredients for success. There is nothing worse than out-of-date, weary-looking materials that have obviously been forgotten. An information professional who is visiting other departments on a regular basis as part of their public relations strategy will ensure that this does not happen.

The work of specialized departments of the library can be a theme of successful displays, if these displays are placed in other departments of the library, as well as in the more usual main entrance or display area. A display policy that incorporates the work of other departments in the authority or organization could be two-way co-operation where all parties benefit. The library could usefully mount displays in social service, planning and health departments taking displays in turn from them to display in relevant library departments or branches.

Some of the most successful public relations ventures have involved encouraging community groups or local businesses or arts organizations to display their activities on library premises. Equally, persuading the likes of banks and building societies, with their main thoroughfare, shop-window frontages, to display library publicity on a regular basis will repay the effort. A bonus in this type of co-operation is that professional help in mounting the display is to hand and security for any valuable materials is built in. In arranging these forms of activity the library is cultivating good relations within the community, in addition to the interest produced by the displays themselves.

Talks and lectures

If the library organizes a programme of themed public talks or lectures by specialist speakers to be held in the library, it needs to be promoted widely. Talks and lectures, lunchtime or evening, will attract a wider audience than just existing library users, as private subscription libraries can attest. They will be enhanced by appropriate displays of library materials and publications.

Equally valuable in public relations activities is to encourage a readiness in library staff to go out and present themselves and their specializations to the myriad groups in the community, who are usually desperate for good speakers. Library staff are not necessarily speaking about their profession in these situations; the library's image will be enhanced if they are seen as interesting people, specialists with something important to say, who happen to be librarians. Encouragement and the line manager's appreciation are not enough if this is to be part of the planned public relations programme. Time for preparation, as well as presentation, should be given and an evaluation made of the audiences and likely and actual results.

The library may well attract new users as a result of the specialist materials supplied to support the theme of the lecture or talk. The nature of the library – public, academic, private subscription, school – and the nature of the programme will determine whether the term 'talk' or 'lecture' is used in publicity.

Similarly 'friends of the library' schemes, in all kinds of libraries, will often recruit new members too.

Open days

Face-to-face interaction is the strongest of all influences on public relations and is discussed further under 'Personal selling' below. Invitations to an open day for those who are influential in the decision-making process to see for themselves will help to focus a case more sharply than a written report alone ever can. Personal invitations will receive a substantial response and even if attendance is not guaranteed, raising awareness is.

An open day or open evening can be particularly successful when the library opens its behind-the-scenes activities to specific market segments. The information centre will not be inviting in the whole world, but an invitation to other heads of departments or key personnel will bear pleasing results. A wide range of companies and organizations, from breweries to nuclear fuel centres, from pencil factories to police stations, are now offering opportunities for the public to see what really happens and to talk to staff. In some cases the numbers of visitors attracted have risen to proportions where specialist staff are employed and entrance fees charged.

Libraries can benefit by targeting particular segments of the market and tailoring the experience accordingly. Potential women returners to work have been targeted particularly successfully by some public libraries, while university 'tasters' have been offered to UK fifth- and sixth-formers, in which the university library has played as substantial a part as the students' union in the public relations programme. One memorable example, which raised the profile of a particular library among its local community, was substantially due to the attendant good publicity. A primary schoolteacher had approached the library on behalf of her pupil library monitors, who had written, in vain, to a popular television programme. The children had asked the programme to 'fix it' for them to visit the biggest library in the world. The university library did not claim even to approach the criterion, but it must have appeared pretty big to the six-year-olds, who were invited to spend a day behind the scenes with the library staff. The children were enchanted, as was the community, as news of the successful day spread.

Publications as promotion

As we saw in Chapter 4, all the types of publication that are products – abstracting and indexing services, local history studies, specialist monographs, calendars, statistical surveys, business reports – are important in enhancing, or otherwise, the image of the library or information centre. An organization or company's in-house journals or newsletters may well be published by the library or information centre; if this is the case, then the fact needs to be proclaimed loudly and not hidden in the typesetting details on the final page. If another department is responsible, articles and items for publication should be fed through steadily so that a presence is maintained in every issue; a regular column could be an aim.

It is important that the member of the library or information centre staff who is given responsibility for this area is given time to collect information from colleagues, and to prepare and present such material. Support is essential from senior management, who must stress to all staff the importance of feeding information and material to their designated colleague.

Annual reports

Annual reports deserve particular attention in promotional terms because of their circulation, readership and, sometimes, legal status.

The information centre will come into its own in the run-up to the publication of its organization's annual report – every department needs its services. The information centre should ensure that it has the same amount of space as every other department in the annual report itself, as well as using the preparation period to emphasize the value and efficiency of the service in the influential quarters of the chairman and the board of directors.

Libraries will more often be expected to produce an annual report on their own account – a perfect opportunity to strengthen value perception in the minds of the decision makers. It is comparatively easy to obtain the annual reports of successful large companies. They are excellent models to emulate in content and presentation. The physical format may well be too expensive to copy, but it is important to present a professional image. The annual report needs to include basic facts and figures, required by legislation or regulation, and they can be forcefully presented using techniques of statistical presentation found in any modern textbook or software package. The report in general can be made more attractive by the use of carefully chosen photographs, a good layout and well-designed typefaces.

It *will* be read if it is written in an accessible style, communicating directly with the target readership. Who are they? What do they require to know? What does the librarian want to draw to their attention? What image of the library does he or she want to strengthen?

The distribution of the annual report can have added value as a public relations exercise if a short, individual memo is attached to the copies designated for specific directors or committee members, drawing their attention to particular points in the report. This has a two-fold effect: it highlights a point where the librarian needs support or appreciation and, secondly, it suggests that the recipients' views are held in high regard – good for public relations.

Stationery

Inculcating awareness of a service needs firm foundations at the policy level and implementation in every detail. Stationery is a simple way to start. For promotional purposes, 'stationery' includes every memo, information sheet, fax, or answer to a query. All must bear the name of the library or information centre; every piece of stationery, including electronic mail, must identify the source.

The use of colour can be considered here too: the yellow pads of the legal profession are recognized by everyone. Choose a colour and use it everywhere. If this sounds expensive for a school library or small information centre, the use of well-designed stick-on labels will help create a unified image.

Consider e-mail colours too in this regard: screens and fonts could carry corporate livery in a standard presentation style very effectively. Care needs to be taken in adding a standard sign-off slogan or quote: they can be very irritating to the recipients.

Recruitment advertisements

Even something as apparently straightforward as a staff recruitment advertisement needs consideration. It is not only those seeking employment who are influenced by the format, wording and place of appearance of such an advertisement – professionals everywhere browse these pages from interest. Increasing use of the internet for recruitment purposes, for personnel seekers and job seekers alike, means that to retain credibility, libraries and information centres must advertise there.

Personal selling

The value of the personal interface with clients, existing and potential, must be emphasized in any promotion strategy. It can quite literally mean knocking on doors: doors of community leaders, company directors, managers in organizations of all kinds, education, industry or government departments. The purpose of a visit, if one is needed as an opening gambit, could be the follow-up to a mailshot, or the introduction of a new service. Visits and information gathering, when repeated at regular frequencies, will aid in building user profiles, identifying needs as well as developing good customer relations. A plan should be prepared, integrated with other elements of the marketing mix: decisions on market segments to be tackled in this way, individuals to be targeted, frequency of visits, who is to do the visiting, and what kinds of follow-up will be arranged.

The value of representation on appropriate committees and groups by the library or information centre staff is discussed in Chapter 4 as part of a planned marketing mix. Welcoming representatives of market segments to participate in working parties or committees of the library and information centre will generate goodwill as well as useful information and support.

All staff, including senior management, need to be convinced of the value of what is coming to be known as 'relationship marketing'; that is, the integration of a quality approach and concern for the user or client, which is capable of building and sustaining a good relationship between the organization and its various publics. Relationship marketing is discussed more fully in Chapter 7.

Direct marketing

Direct marketing is the use of non-media advertising to introduce products or services by mail, including electronic, or telephone. Librarians and information professionals may think direct marketing is inappropriate and furthermore, too expensive for them to consider. E-mail is changing the perception of the latter but it is sensible to consider the marketing effectiveness of all direct marketing methods before ruling any out. Sponsorship could be sought for mailings over a period or for specific purposes and would give an opportunity for market research to prove the value of this marketing method.

Databases

The communications-mix strategy must look to the building-up and *maintenance* of databases of existing users and potential users as part of the overall marketing information system. A tailor-made database, able to process user information and characteristics, will aid the effective implementation of marketing strategies considerably. The cost of setting up and maintenance, if it is planned well, will be offset by the effectiveness of direct targeting of required segments. Existing databases, within an organization and from external sources, should be investigated, as they may very well serve specific purposes cost-effectively. *It is absolutely crucial to keep the database current.* The resource implications are substantial, but an inaccurate, out-of-date database will cost more in the long run, gain enemies and damage the image you want to give of a professional, efficient, caring organization.

The majority of libraries do not currently use registration efficiently, but it can be a way of gathering useful details for the database. Market information can also be collected initially from personnel departments. Characteristics should be added as the user responds to approaches, so that future mailshots or contact with the user can be tailored even more effectively to their needs. Age discrimination legislation in some countries precludes date of birth questions, but most users would be happy indicating an age category and giving some indication of subject interests and family position. E-mail addresses can be completed or not as the user wishes. Users must be given the opportunity to opt out of receiving marketing communications.

Data protection legislation is complex and it is not enough to rely on the legal department of the authority or organization: librarians and information professionals must keep abreast of changes in legislation and be aware of differences across frontiers where appropriate. Data protection legislation is looked at again in Chapter 7.

Telephone marketing

An information centre introducing new services of value to existing clients within a very small segment of their market will have good personal relations in all likelihood, and telephone contact will be feasible and effective.

Telephone marketing is not recommended as the most cost-effective method of reaching potential users for libraries and information centres in other cases, although other service industries such as the financial and insurance sectors do use it extensively and effectively and the call centre explosion is achieving legendary proportions.

Direct mail

Direct mail, on the other hand, places promotional literature and information in the hands of those whom the library or information centre wishes to reach, and gives the target group time to consider the information contained. The effectiveness of the mailshot can be evaluated via the return of the forms, coupons or vouchers that were included for action or an e-mail response. It is often feasible for a library to cut costs by including literature in a mailshot from the parent organization. It can also add credibility to a range of quality services on offer. What should almost go without saying is that this depends on co-operation with and knowledge of what the organization and other departments are planning – good internal public relations.

A mailshot in the relevant geographical areas could, for example, introduce a new mobile library service quickly, and the information on days and times could be kept for reference – an ongoing reminder. New services for part-time students can be promoted most effectively by contacting them directly by mail, and internal mail will keep costs down. Junk mail will always go where it deserves, in the bin, but a personally addressed letter or e-mail, with an attractive leaflet or design, obviously of interest because the characteristics and needs of the recipient have been carefully judged, will attract attention and provoke action. The sheer novelty of receiving a communication of this kind from the public library is likely to provoke interest and action. Birthday cards can be sent to children, for example, by the public library. A secondary school was successful in increasing school rolls when it sent birthday cards to the younger brothers and sisters of pupils in the school. CD-

ROM production is now so cheap that an information centre could consider it as a medium for the distribution by mail of sample information.

E-mail marketing

E-mail deserves much more serious attention than it is currently given. Everyday, internal e-mail communication is as important to internal marketing as e-mail used to reach target segments and build customer relationships.

The best work, in a field surprisingly short on good advice, comes from Sterne and Priore (2000). Their advice is practical and their style accessible, for example, on E-mail Header and Subject: 16% of users delete unknown senders, although 17% will open a communication from a recognized company or organization. So identify the library or information centre, use action words and suggest this e-mail will solve problems (ibid., 143–7). They quote Mark Gibbs on emoticons or smileys: 'these were once funny, but now they have descended to the nether regions of cultural hell alongside "Precious Moments" figurines and Day-Glo velvet pictures of Elvis.'

The clear marketing message is: don't just hit the reply button – every communication is a marketing opportunity and should be treated accordingly.

The major difference in direct marketing in the electronic context is that the user opts in rather than opting out. *Permission marketing* is discussed in Chapter 7. It refers to the way in which a user or client must give, along with their details, often via online registration forms, their explicit permission to be contacted with marketing communications, the newsletters, offers, updates on services, that will come to them online thereafter. Market segmentation is made that much easier as a result of this process.

AIDA

The AIDA marketing concept of Awareness, Interest, Desire and Action (see above) is particularly appropriate to direct marketing. The personal approach, the immediate laying out of benefits for the recipient and the need for quick response action are the hallmarks of good direct marketing. Follow-up to an initial approach is vital, a relationship is forming. A second letter, reinforcing the message of the first, can follow up flyers, brochures and offers made by post.

Press releases and press conferences

A *press conference* is no more than a meeting to which representatives of the media have been invited to learn of a major event or news item. The media are usually provided with written support material, sometimes photographs, and the opportunity to question key figures involved in what is being drawn to their attention.

A *press briefing* will not be used by libraries and information centres as a method of relating with the media. It is used in regular, sometimes daily, circumstances when a government, organization or company wishes to keep the media up to date with a changing situation and the media meet a spokesperson who issues news bulletins and is prepared to answer questions.

A *press release* is a written communication sent to a selected set of press and broadcasting media. It can be sent by post, fax or electronic mail. A press release may sometimes be called a news release, but very often the communication, while being of interest, could not properly be called news.

The use of these publicity methods must be assessed against the value of paid-for advertising (see the section 'Promotion/User communication' in Chapter 4). Press releases and personal cultivation of media relationships are highly recommended: they will quickly provide good results and over time reap extensive dividends. But remember that when the library or information service pays for advertising there is control over what appears in content and over the desired format. There is no control at all over how the media might use information sent as a press release, if indeed it is used at all.

A well-presented press release, relevant to readers or viewers or listeners, that is timely, interesting and accurate, preferably with local content of some description for the local media, will have every chance of being used. If it's good enough, it may be used more than once by the same medium: the provincial press with multiple editions by geographical area and weekend magazines are prime examples of having two bites at the cherry.

Content and presentation

The communication skills of librarians and information professionals will lead them quickly to success in seeing their efforts published. The choice of media to which the press release might be sent will vary according to the target markets aimed at by the library or information centre. Here is a checklist of what to include in a professional press release:

- source of release
- heading/title
- first line hook
- what it's all about
- why it's important
- when it's happening
- who is involved
- quote from somebody relevant
- contact details.

e-media releases

As a result of the huge take-up of information technology by the media, press releases sent by e-mail are much more acceptable than they once were, and in some media the norm. Initially frowned upon, it is now easy for journalists to edit or insert electronic copy sent in this way. The same rules apply to all press releases, but it is important that the e-mail format press release is sent to the appropriate e-mail address as advised by the newspaper or journal. (It is worth repeating that for recipients not to be aware of everybody else on the distribution list use of the Bcc: box is recommended, not To: or Cc:.)

E-mail links for contact names should be given. Hyperlinks can also be provided to online reports and further information via the website of the library or information centre. Transfer to an HTML file for web purposes before sending the media release is important and it is advisable to provide an archive of press releases accessible, via the website of the library or information centre.

It is also possible to pay for media release services, where a web company will distribute press (media) releases to targeted media journalists, on behalf of the library or information centre, via e-mail. Yahoo! is one of the search services available that gives access to archived press releases, useful for examples, as well as information, and it is important that the library and information centre submits their archive of press releases for inclusion.

Presentation

When advertising new products, companies have used a variety of press release formats, for example champagne bottles with the message on the label. Totally unimpressed, media recipients will drink the champagne and put the bottle in the bin or more likely send the bottle to a deserving local cause.

It is essential to produce a professional, effective, single page of copy on good-quality paper, or via e-mail, well presented with a good clear layout. Only one side of the paper should be used, or screen-sized information by e-mail; double spacing and a clear typeface are imperative for both methods.

It is advisable to consider specially printed stationery headed Press Release, since even a small mailing list contacted regularly soon warrants it. It is then absolutely clear what this communication is and it will be treated accordingly. Another factor to consider is that using the stationery of the authority or the parent organization will not necessarily make it clear that the press release has come from the library or the information centre. If the organization's policy is to control all releases centrally, building good relations with the relevant department is essential to ensure that there is a steady flow of information regarding the library or information service reaching the media.

The library or information centre should be identified with an address, telephone number and URL (see also advice on contact details below).

The date of issue of the press release should be accompanied by a highlighted, identified embargo date if the information is not to be released before a certain time and date.

The heading needs to stand out clearly and state in a simple and straightforward way what the press release is about. Many hundreds of press releases are received by media professionals in the course of a week; a decision on whether to pass on to the next stage or bin the release will often depend on the heading. It should not be a catchy headline, that is the sub-editor or journalists' job, and they do not take kindly to what may have appeared very witty at the time it was penned, but will not appeal to their particular readership.

Interest needs to be caught immediately, so the equivalent to new, innovative, original, needs to be in the first line, alongside the local connection for the local media where possible. The rest of the information should be brief, to the point, and cover essential details of issue, venue, date, time and price if relevant. The chances of the press release being used will be enhanced by a quote from a named person, with a description of who they are. In print it sounds as if the person has actually been interviewed, a plus point for the desk-bound journalist. It is vital to check with the person 'quoted' that they are happy to say what you would like them to, before the release goes to the media.

The use of the word 'ends' at the end of the information content is a useful device, but it is not the end of the press release.

Contact details

A contact for further information should always be given. The contact should be a named person and the title and job or status should also be given, as any information or comment which that person gives can then be seen in context. Naturally, the contact person needs to be an authoritative and good source of information, and also someone who is articulate and will enhance the image of the library or information service. Information on contact should contain telephone numbers (and times available, if different from normal office hours) and e-mail address.

Opportunities for the media to do interviews, take photographs or film activities can be indicated, where a special session is arranged. In addition, the contact person needs to be prepared on the practical considerations of such requests from the media if other staff or the public would be involved.

Photographs to accompany a press release are more popular today, given the ease of technical reproduction, but a good picture is still a rarity. Where a photograph is used, it must be married to the press release. A label on the back must give the name of the library or information service, press release heading and date. The names of people in the photograph must be in order, indicating where they are, for example, left to right, front row, back row. Copyright requirements need to be taken into account and the photographer may require a credit if the photograph is used.

Timing

The date for sending out a press release needs careful consideration. Opportunities of wide coverage before and at the time of an event will be maximized with a well-timed press release. Too early and the impact will be dissipated, too late and the opportunity has been lost. Never send information after the event: news editors are not interested in what has been and gone. Finally, collect all the press cuttings, record the broadcasts, copy the e-mail responses and send copies to key influential decision makers.

Sample press releases (see pages 111 and 112)

The first sample press release gives an example of very straightforward information, aimed at the local market. It is about a public library's opening hours over a holiday period and a small promotional exercise that adds two hours per week, over three weeks, to opening hours. The photo opportunities for television coverage as well as press media are evident, especially as broadcasters are looking for new child angles at Christmas.

The second sample is meant for release by e-mail and answers the current need for internet users to hear about themselves. Net market research shows that news about research is popular with internet users, particularly when gender distinctions are discussed, and likely to be used by internet media.

Note: *Names and information in the sample press releases are completely fictitious.*

Bridgetown Arts and Recreation
Bridgetown Libraries
Bridgetown Central Library
Bridge Street
Bridgetown
ME3 5ST

Press Release

Date of release: immediate [actual date]

Late night opening: new library service
For the first time, Bridgetown Libraries will open their doors until 10pm on Tuesday nights in December during the run-up to Christmas. Jennifer Noble, Bridgetown Director of Arts and Recreation, says:

> People work and shop around the clock. We wanted to give them the opportunity to choose their books, music and videos, give them ideas for Christmas presents and activities and be available for any queries at times best suited to them. It is an experiment which the libraries hope to continue when we see how successful it is.

The borough libraries will be open as usual apart from Christmas Day, Boxing Day and January 1st.

A special programme of children's activities, craft fairs and displays of work by local artists will run from December 8th to January 6th.

Details are available from any branch library (Tel: 0102 345 6789) or the Libraries' website at **www.bridgetown.arts.libraries.org.uk**

END

Contact for further information:
Jeremy Hall
Heritage Librarian
Bridgetown Central Library
Bridge Street
Bridgetown ME3 5ST
Tel: 0102 345 6789
Fax: 0102 345 6780
E:mail: j.hall@bridgetown.gov.uk

Press release 1

From: Badger Pharmaceuticals Information Sources
Subject: New internet research from pharmaceutical industry

Media Release

Date of release: immediate [actual date]

New research on internet users in pharmaceuticals

New research from the Association of Pharmaceutical Professionals shows the internet to be the first source from choice for researchers in the pharmaceutical industry when seeking information.

Barbara Brown, President of the APP, welcomed the research, saying 'We see this research as demonstrating how much professionals in the pharmaceutical industry are prepared to share their findings and co-operate with colleagues. It is part of our professional ethical code that we maintain the highest standards of professional practice in taking pharmaceutical research forward.'

A significant factor in the research showed that male researchers were twice as likely as female researchers to contact colleagues via the internet to follow up information.

The report can be accessed via the Association of Pharmaceutical Professionals website at **www.pharmaceuticals-professionals.org.uk**

END

Contact for further information:
Samantha Robson
Badger Pharmaceuticals Information Sources
Information Manager
Bristham BE3 4ST
Tel:+44 (0)103 10 234 5678
E-mail: sam.robson@badgerpharm.com

Press release 2

References and further reading

Aslib (1992) *Sponsorship in libraries*, vol. 1, Report and survey.

Barrett, G. (1995) *Forensic marketing: optimizing results from marketing communication, the essential guide*, McGraw-Hill.

Brassington, F. and Pettit, S. (2000) *Principles of marketing*, 2nd edn, Pitman Publishing.

Cannon, T. (1996) *Basic marketing*, 4th edn, Cassell.

Chisnall, P. M. (2001) *Marketing research*, 6th edn, McGraw-Hill.

Colley, R. H. (1961) *Defining advertising goals for measured advertising results*, Association of National Advertisers.

Cutlip, S. M., Center, A. H. and Broom, G. M. (2000) *Effective public relations*, 8th edn, Prentice Hall.

Fill, C. (1999) *Marketing communication: framework, theories and application*, 2nd edn, Prentice Hall.

Haig, M. (2000) *e-pr: the essential guide to public relations on the internet*, Kogan Page.

Hardaker, G. and Graham, G. (2001) *Wired marketing*, John Wiley and Sons.

Harrington, R. (2001) Keynote speech, *11th European Business Conference*, (March), London and New York, Task Force Pro Libra, not yet published.

Janal, D. S. (2000) *Dan Janal's guide to marketing on the internet*, John Wiley and Sons.

Jefkins, F. (1994) *Public relations techniques*, 2nd edn, Butterworth-Heinemann.

Jefkins, F. (2000) *Advertising*, 4th edn, revised and edited by D. Yadin, Pearson Education.

Kotler, P. (1999) *Kotler on marketing*, The Free Press.

Kotler, P. and Andreasen, A. A. (1996) *Strategic marketing for non-profit organizations*, Prentice Hall.

Marshall, N. J. (2001) Public relations in academic libraries: a descriptive analysis, *Journal of Academic Librarianship*, **27** (2), 116–21.

Moloney, K. (2000) *Rethinking public relations: the spin and the substance*, Routledge.

Percy, L., Rossiter, J. R. and Elliott, R. (2001) *Strategic advertising management*, Oxford University Press.

Rossiter, J. R. and Bellman, S. (1999) A proposed model for explaining and measuring web ad effectiveness, *Journal of Current Issues and Research in Advertising*, **21** (1), 13–31.

Rossiter, J. R. and Percy, L. (1997) *Advertising communication and promotion management*, McGraw-Hill.

Seybold, P. (2001) *The customer revolution*, Random House.

Smith, P. R. (1998) *Marketing communication: an integrated approach*, Kogan Page.

Sterne, J. and Priore, A. (2000) *Email marketing*, John Wiley and Sons.

Tapp, A. (2001) *Principles of direct and database marketing*, 2nd edn, Pearson Education.

Terry, F. (2001) Patents reveal secrets of competitors, *Sunday Times*, (25 November), 15.

White, J. and Mazur, L. (1995) *Strategic communications management: making public relations work*, Addison-Wesley.

Wilson, R. M. S. and Gilligan, C. with Howsden, M. (1995) *Strategic marketing management*, Butterworth-Heinemann.

Wolfe, L. A. (1997) *Library public relations, promotion and communications*, Neal-Schumann.

6

Market segmentation

Essentially, segmentation is the division of the library or information centre's market into smaller, more manageable, groups that have like characteristics. Marketing mixes can be fine tuned to serve the needs of these groups or segments and marketing communications targeted more precisely. The practice of segmenting markets leads to better use of resources since those resources can be targeted with maximum effectiveness.

The objectives of this chapter are:

- to demonstrate the benefits of segmenting a market into more manageable groups
- to identify the methods of segmenting markets for marketing purposes: geographic, demographic, behavioural, psychographic and lifestyle
- to explore how segmentation affects marketing-mix decisions and practice for libraries and information centres
- to explore how libraries and information centres can differentiate their product for the target market.

Mass-marketing or undifferentiated marketing can work, if a product or service has features acceptable to a wide variety of users, but it is less and less common as users make more sophisticated demands and have a higher expectancy of tailor-made service. Major companies that relied on standard products for years now adopt new product features and packaging to target particular markets: breakfast cereals come packaged for children, for health-aware adults, those who want to slim and customers wanting a different variety every day.

Market segmentation can group the library's users or information centre's clients into target markets with similar characteristics, needs and wants. Specific marketing mixes can then be tailored to the requirements of the different market segments, hence *differentiated marketing*.

Characteristics of segmentation

A market segment needs to satisfy the following criteria if it is to be targeted successfully:

- The segment should be *homogenous*, i.e. the characteristic variables of the group need to be identifiable and strong enough to warrant different treatment.
- The segment needs to be *accessible* for targeting to succeed. An identifiable segment may be available only at particular times, student populations in term-time, twilight shift workers, etc.
- The segment size should be *measurable* and justify targeting. This does not always mean large numbers, but cost effectiveness should be a primary question for librarians and information managers. In a constantly changing world, perception of size viability will change constantly and also, in mission statement terms, a duty of responsibility may enforce targeting a segment otherwise considered not to be cost effective.

Some marketers would add appropriateness and stability to the list of criteria; that is, appropriate to the organization's objectives and resources, and stability in the sense that the segment's future behaviour might be predicted. Stability is almost an unlooked-for luxury today as the macro-environment changes and influences all markets profoundly.

The librarian or information professional aims at segmenting their market into groups which can be served effectively and also help to develop the service. Appropriate or natural segments will be identified as prime targets when there is a positive answer to the following questions:

- Awareness – can they be made aware successfully?
- Availability – can the service be made available to them effectively?
- Affordability – can the segment afford to use the service?
- Acceptability – can the service be made more acceptable to them?

Internet segmentation

The internet market is showing different characteristics of segmentation from the general population (Chaffey et al., 2000, 37) as the nature of the medium dictates the market, but as take-up increases the differences will dissolve. Home use currently is restricted to those with personal computers, interactive digital television services via cable or satellite and mobile phones with web facilities, while other users have access in the work or education sectors or via their public libraries.

Internet users are characterized by 'itchy finger syndrome – an overwhelming desire to click on a mouse at least once every fifteen seconds' (Haig, 2000, 40), so that interactive websites, bulletin boards and chat and e-mail facilities are important to them.

Bickerton, Bickerton and Pardesi (1996) used lifestyle segmentation to classify internet users into: techno-lusters, academic buffs, knowledge traders, hobbyists, home users and get aheads. The latter used the internet and e-mail as a lifestyle accessory. They are all potential market segments for libraries and information services and it is plain that the following will be just as valid for the internet market.

Methods of segmentation

The methods of dividing the market into segments are many and often it is a combination of methods that leads to success. Markets were hitherto divided most commonly by geographic, demographic and benefit variables or usage rates. Geodemographic, behavioural and psychographic variables add complexity but greatly enhance targeting success.

Help is available in commercially available software and numerous companies make segmentation their core business. A useful starting point for librarians and information professionals would be McDonald and Dunbar's (1995) step-by-step manual on market segmentation, which concentrates on the commercial sector but is straightforward on concepts with a multitude of practical actions to aim for. The manual is accompanied by software, The Market Segment Master.

Geographic segmentation

Geographic segmentation by country, region, county or city, when used alone, will give relatively simple targets on a scale so large that one might as well be mass-marketing for libraries and information services.

Regional preferences, for example, tend to show up in taste differences, both aesthetic and in consumption. Regional cultures and practices should be taken into account not only by public librarians, but also by the information professionals working in pan-global companies and organizations where their regions are the regions of the world.

Demographic segmentation

Demographic segmentation divides markets according to demographic variables such as age, sex, income, occupation, race, nationality, religion, education, family size and family lifecycle stage.

The traditional family lifecycle stages defined by Wells and Gubar (1966) fit less easily now when sweeping changes in society have removed many of the traditional roles and norms. The characteristics of the groups they define bear consideration even so:

1 *Bachelor stage – young, single, living at home.* Likely to use libraries and information services for leisure, career information and education.

2 *Newly married couples – young, no children*. These days may not be married, but home and consumer oriented anyway; they could well use libraries to enhance their home and leisure activities or career promotion potential.

3 *Full nest 1 – youngest child under six*. Not much disposable income; will need information services to help in coping with family situation and libraries could provide accessible leisure services, as well as information. A creche in the library would help. Need materials about child development as well as books and other materials for their children.

4 *Full nest 2 – youngest child six or over*. Children's services in public libraries are an obvious draw. The female partner may consider returning to work full time; the library will be an invaluable source of information on opportunities, education and self-development needed.

5 *Full nest 3 – older couples with dependent children*. The children are still at home or perhaps away in first jobs or higher education. Either way, money is not freely available and a wide range of library and information services will be appropriate to parents and children.

6 *Empty nest 1 – older couples, children not living at home, head of the household still working*. Income at its peak; there will be a call for different types of information, and different sources will be used. More sophisticated leisure pursuits, often expensive, will compete with library services.

7 *Empty nest 2 – older couples, head of the household retired*. Retired early or redundant; either way there is a drop in income and libraries can grasp new opportunities to attract an articulate and supportive group.

8 *Solitary survivor in the workforce*. Income may be relatively high; information services will support a new, perhaps enforced, set of perceptions. More likely to need specialized information on financial matters, hobbies or pursuits.

9 *Solitary survivor, retired*. Will need attention and security; librarians need to remind themselves of Maslow's (1987) concept of drives (discussed later in this chapter under 'User adoption').

Geodemographic segmentation

Geodemographic systems classify users according to where they live, on the basis that people living in a particular type of dwelling in a specific neighbourhood are likely to exhibit economic, social and lifestyle similarities.

The ACORN system (A Classification of Residential Neighbourhoods) is one of the best known. It is based on census enumeration districts plus demographic, housing and social variables. Examples from the ACORN classification include: modern family housing, higher incomes; better-off council estates; high-status, non-family areas; and multiracial areas. SAGACITY groupings, formulated by Research Services, are also much used. They divide the lifecycle into dependent, pre-family, family and late, further subdivided by income and occupation. Other systems include MOSAIC from CCN, Infolink's DEFINE, and PIN from PINPOINT Analysis. All of these systems claim only to reach the segments characterized by a clear set of demographic variables.

People do have different aspirations as well as behaviour patterns as they move through life. Occupation today, for example, as a social classification, is no predictor of real income or lifestyle, particularly in terms of family members, who may differ widely from each other in socioeconomic characteristics. Despite their obvious problems, the traditional social class grades are given here because they are still widely used:

Class A:	upper middle class – higher managerial or professional
Class B:	middle class – middle to senior management
Class Cl:	lower middle class – junior management; supervisory or clerical grades
Class C2:	skilled working class – manual trades
Class D:	working class – semi- and unskilled workers
Class E:	pensioners – those on the breadline, dependent on state benefits.

Librarians and information professionals need to take care not to make assumptions in targeting markets segmented in this way. The UK Market

Research Society's guide to socioeconomic status is based on occupation, qualifications and responsibility. Bank managers appear with admirals, chief constables, bishops and homeopaths, among others, at A; B includes archdeacons, secondary-school teachers, senior engineers and ballistics experts; Cl intriguingly includes all announcers – television, radio or station platform – cardiographers, police constables, magicians and monks; C2 sees carpenters with deep-sea divers and AA patrolmen; D encompasses the dustman (not refuse collector), nursemaid and rat catcher.

Demographic trends are predicting an ever-expanding population of the third age, defined in the UK as 50 to 70 years old, but some European countries stretch the boundaries. It does make sense for the public library to look at the needs of that sector, in political and economic as well as humanitarian terms. An articulate and knowledgeable sector of the community with a lively interest in public affairs, they can be harnessed for support purposes if the library offers sufficient benefits to them. Also, since they are likely to have disposable income – mortgages paid off, family gone from home – profit-making services could be aimed at them.

The new underclasses, identified, sadly, in most countries today, do not find a place in the majority of models. They would need very different methods of outreach and there is a real need for research into potential methods, outcomes and benefits.

Behaviourial segmentation

Behavioural segmentation differentiates target markets according to usage rates, willingness to innovate or user perception of benefit. Usage rates will often be classified as volume segmentation by consumer product companies, who will endeavour to attract non-users to become first-time users and to persuade light users to become heavy users.

While librarians and information professionals will often have very similar aims, it is probably more valuable to think of users in benefit terms rather than quantitative terms. Any analysis of benefits sought and satisfied will undoubtedly demonstrate instances of benefits sought but unsatisfied, which could be remedied effectively. Examples of benefits for library or information service users might be, for instance, improved proficiency in a hobby or interest, more effective use of leisure time, better grades in academic courses, more effective use of research funding or simply being better informed.

Lifestyle segmentation

Research on personality differences has proved less conclusive than lifestyle categorization, for which numerous models now exist. Lifestyle segmentation attempts to profile a person's way of living and acting. People coming from the same social group, having the same level of education and even same type of occupation may well have different activities and interests. Palmer (2001) suggests that service organizations look to the loyalty card schemes of retailers, where the patterns of customer spending, what, when and how much, are recorded to better target customers in future with offers of interest to them. Borrowing or request patterns could be used in a similar way.

VALS and VALS2 (see Mitchell, 1983) were developed in the United States at the Stanford Research Institute. The VALS approach, **V**alues **A**nd **L**ifestyle **S**egmentation, classifies the population into a number of categories (formerly nine, now eight) including: *sustainers*, who are disadvantaged but fighting hard to escape; *belongers*, who are conventional, nostalgic, generally reluctant to experiment; *achievers*, who make things happen and enjoy life; and the *societally conscious*, who have a marked sense of social responsibility. The theory maintains that as people move through life they act according to how they are needs driven, whether external acclaim is important to them (hence the rise in the importance of branding) or the satisfaction of individual need is of prime importance. The marketing message needs to be couched differently for the separate segments as a consequence.

The role of the librarian and information professional must be to act as facilitator to all of the lifestyle categories, to help each of them cope with the increasing complexities of the information world.

Psychographic segmentation

The personal, psychological, social and cultural factors that govern user behaviour are beyond the control of the librarian or information professional, who nevertheless needs to be aware of their likely impact and influence on the use of services offered. High-technology information centres today will have real coffee wafting at you as you enter, although it may well be decaffeinated to let you recognize the human face of information technology.

Piirto (1991) is hailed by David Statt (1997) as 'the leading authority on the practical applications of psychographics'. Statt's own work takes some beating. *Understanding the consumer: a psychological approach* is one of the most accessible, and funny, texts available in this area. He includes Mildred, the militant mother, Thelma, the old-fashioned traditionalist and Candice, the chic subversive. Most consumer behaviour texts would include the same group types – they come from the respected advertising agency Needham, Harper and Steers – but it is Statt who brings them to life. Statt also includes the salutary tale of the US company Combat. Combat tried to persuade female customers in the Southern states to buy a cleaner, more hygienic way of killing cockroaches. Their customers preferred the traditional spray. Why? Market research showed that the women, when asked to draw the cockroaches and write about their feelings towards them, were clearly writing about the men in their lives. 'Killing the roaches with a bug spray and watching them squirm and die allowed the women to express their hostility toward men and it also allowed them a feeling of power and control' (Statt, 1997, 107). How do users perceive their information suppliers?

Blackwell, Miniard and Engel (2001) look closely at the impact of technology on consumer behaviour in their work, *Consumer behavior*, now in its ninth edition. There is a useful website to accompany the text (linked to the publisher's website) where the authors offer to respond to questions and comment.

Faison (1980) on motivation in marketing is still to be recommended for the splendid range of examples and balance of received opinion and tongue-in-cheek style. Early examples from marketing history show how, for example, the introduction of cake mixes to the market was set back, since subconsciously a woman treated baking a cake like giving birth: instant mixes removed the creative process. Instant coffee was not well received initially, because it carried connotations of laziness, as if users could not be bothered to produce the real thing.

The library visit is not seen to be in the same perception category as going to the gym, to a concert, to the theatre, to a football match. Why not? We need to examine the motivational factors as closely as the commercial sector examining coffee or cockroach killer purchases.

Abraham Maslow's (1987) classic work on personality and motivation is helpful to the librarian and information professional. He maintained that individuals are driven by a set of needs, hierarchical in structure. They are physiological, safety, social, esteem and self-actualization needs. Maslow's theory applies not only to users: library and information service personnel have the same structure of needs too.

Physiological needs

Legislation on ease of access has reduced much of the agony for the disabled, but where is the provision for the rest of society? Basic needs, thankfully, are now being catered for in larger public libraries, but it is the smaller branches that are not near to accommodating shops or other facilities, which need lavatories, babies' feeding and changing areas, a source of food and drink, and simply somewhere to sit comfortably. The odd low-slung armchair, uncomfortable to get out of if you are elderly, infirm or weighed down by care is not the answer. Why are there no facilities for leaving coats and bags safely in public libraries? Academic libraries, national libraries, continental supermarkets can do it. Increased user satisfaction and a probable growth in use can counter the argument of staff and space.

Security and safety needs

Individuals seek physical and mental protection and security. A welcoming atmosphere does much to reduce insecurity and raise confidence in users. Information centres, because of the very nature of their often highly specialized work, need particularly to seek to reduce users' potential anxiety.

Where a public library branch is in a shopping centre, deserted at night, then it makes little sense to put users, and staff, at potential risk by operating in the late evening. Health and safety legislation has forced attention to poor flooring, electrics and other hazards. High, over-packed shelving should never be seen; hot coffee machines need to be away from inquisitive fingers; temperature controls should not need someone with an engineering degree to operate them.

Allied to an understanding of the market segment's needs, often it is common sense that is most needed.

Social needs

A sense of belonging is important to all of us. The public library has the opportunity to serve an individual from the very earliest age, through growing up and becoming independent, to maturity and onwards. The feeling that the user is a member of a welcoming club needs to be fostered. A leaflet proclaiming 'Join the Club' attracted many new users in one public library authority. Formal registration can be made more of an event than the usual completion of a form and receipt of a ticket. How many libraries send out invitations to events, or perhaps offer benefits for increased use? Are there 'welcome to the library' packages for newcomers to the area? Housing departments and associations, estate agents, churches and schools can all be useful intermediaries for the distribution of such packages. An introduction to a named member of staff who can do a mini induction for new users will impress newcomers to a company as well as geographical area.

How is it made obvious that staff are willing to share their knowledge and discuss the materials they have lovingly selected, organized and are now happy to see being used? How are users made to feel that their contributions are welcome? School libraries publish pupils' book reviews: where are their counterparts for the adult user and what encouragement is there for library-based activities for adults? Of course, it is valuable to have the local knitting or sewing group or social-work surgery on library premises, but could there not be a sharing of views and perhaps even formalized help in material selection procedures?

The information centre will normally have a restricted membership and the opportunity to know users and build up a rapport with them is thus much easier. Equally academic subject librarians, college librarians and subscription-library staff must foster relationships.

Esteem needs

Customer care is the watchword in both public and private sectors as we move into the service age of the 21st century. The client is firmly at the centre of missions and strategic policies; libraries and information services must demonstrate this constantly and consistently if they are to succeed.

The need to feel that one is respected as a person is vital to an individual's concept of self. Empowerment of individuals became the creed of the 1990s. Librarians and information professionals can aid in empowering individuals in society, supplying the fuel of knowledge for that empowerment.

Self-actualization

Self-actualization refers to the potential in all of us waiting to be realized. Maslow (1987, 134) argues that this is a stage where the individual self has matured to such an extent that, while outer conventions are adhered to, the individual is drawing on inner sources of strength, living in 'the widest possible frame of reference'. It was Maslow's belief that it would be only a small proportion of the population who would reach this stage. Should Maslow be right, would not a huge range of information sources to illuminate the universal view be needed by such individuals?

User adoption

There are definable stages in the user-adoption process that must be taken into account in planning communication and promotion strategies. The stages are:

- Awareness – the potential user may have heard that a service exists, but does not know exactly what it offers, or where and when it is available.
- Interest – there is some kind of stimulation to seek more information.
- Risk appraisal – the user considers the benefits or disadvantages of trying the service.
- Experimentation – the user will make initial use of the service if it is offered on trial and not likely to take too much time, effort or expense.
- Adoption – the user makes regular and full use of the service.

Librarians and information professionals need to consider how potential users can be moved on through the stages to successful adoption. A targeted mail-shot may send further information and some form of incentive to move users from interest to experiment. Students considering new, late opening hours at their campus library might be tempted by free coffee and a regular bus service back to their halls of residence. Any subscription service could offer an introductory period at reduced rates. In the UK, a northern public library service distributed books at particular fairs and festivals, only asking that they be returned to the nearest branch library at the readers' convenience; a 75% increase in membership ensued.

The theory of *diffusion of innovation* describes user behaviour and how a product or service, an innovation in the market, is accepted.

Librarians and information professionals will find it valuable to consider user differences in terms of readiness to innovate, i.e. to accept or adopt a new idea or service. There are distinct differences in the ways in which people are receptive and willing to adopt new ideas and it is an additional gloss to add to the segmentation matrix. Each library or information service will be able to identify its own group of highly influential users who are most likely to aid the diffusion process, that is, spread the idea of using the service by example.

Rogers (1983) classified groups for this purpose as Innovators; Early Adopters; Early Majority Adopters; Late Majority Adopters; and Laggards.

The information-seeking behaviour of each group has distinctive characteristics.

Innovators are that very small percentage of the population, 2.5% according to Rogers, who will always be the first to try a new service. They tend to be younger than Late Majority Adopters, have a more favourable financial and social status and are much more likely to use a wider range of impersonal information sources. Always in the vanguard, they will look for new developments and will want to be the first to know and to act, thus they are highly unlikely to seek information from friends or colleagues.

Early Adopters (only 13.5% of the population) are not so keen to take risks: they would consider options carefully, seek out and use many information sources. They are opinion leaders in their community and their social relationships are wide and well developed.

Early Majority Adopters, the next category and much larger (34% of the population), are more cautious, would expect to have a good foundation of knowledge, and would adopt a new idea or service before the average person. Early Majority Adopters operate in a more deliberate fashion than Early Adopters and would not willingly take the lead, while Late Majority Adopters (a further 34% of the population) are reluctant to try something until it has been well proven.

The *Laggards* (a much smaller group at 16% of the population) are very suspicious of change, will not adopt a service until it is the traditional thing to do, and indeed may only start to use a service at a point when the organization is about to start something else.

The different segments of the adopter classifications require different methods of communication and types of information provision. Demographics and lifestyle data can help identify the users more likely to take up a new service quickly. The information centre, college or school library, where relationships are likely to be personalized, will segment users with a view to the type and amount of information they need on the new service at appropriate points of the service lifecycle.

Creating product differentiation

The essence of marketing communication is to inform the user or client, and to ensure that they move from merely being aware of a product or service to actual use.

Barrett (1995, 180) says there are three generic questions to ask in communicating with the selected market:

- What do we want them to know?
- What do we want them to feel?
- What do we want them to do?

The advertising manager who had 'Quaker Oats' carved on the white cliffs of Dover, in letters so large they could be read in France, knew the answers. Quaker Oats had to remove the letters, such was the outcry, but their product had become a household name.

Marketing communication theory has come a long way since those early days, when it was believed that repeating the product name endlessly would lead to familiarity and, therefore, greater sales. Promotional mix was a term not yet coined. Repetition, in fact, does still work well, but 'promotion includes all the activities the company undertakes to communicate and promote its products to the target market' (Kotler, 2000, 87). What, however, if the library or information service has products of similar merit to the competition? The target segments will need to be persuaded of the benefits and also the added value to them of using the services of the library or information centre and not the competition. The marketing mix will have to be very finely tuned to the segment characteristics.

This is where advertising comes in. It is important that the librarian or information professional controls marketing communications so that the client, or user group, responds to the product or service benefits and not to the blandishments of emotional or attractive advertising. To put it another way, the delivery on promises made, explicitly or implicitly, in marketing communications, is paramount. In the UK, the Advertising Standards Authority monitors the truth of advertising copy today, thus curbing some of the wildly excessive claims of the past, but creativity is still very much the name of the game, and the product or service can easily get lost in advertisements that are mini works of art. 'Current ads reflect radical changes in our technologies and media, our social and economic relations, our sense of personal and group identity' (Cook, 1992, xv). The real challenge lies in targeting markets where competition is fierce and there is little or no difference between the products and services on offer for the same segments (Hammond, Ehrenberg and Goodhardt, 1996). There are few advertisements that highlight the uniqueness of product or service. The USP – unique selling proposition – is quite rare; in fact, most producers of goods or providers of services are, like librarians and information professionals, in a competitive world of like-products and services.

The psychology of advertising

Where physical and objective differentiation between products and services is small or non-existent, the major role of promotion must be to create and develop some subjective or cultural meaning for them. The client, customer or user must be persuaded to use and go on using the particular library or service in the face of competition from similar offerings from other organizations. The prosaic Milward, the sewing needle manufacturer, might repeat the company name forever, but not until their sewing needles became 'crafty needles' and a subjective traditional dimension, 'quality needlemakers since 1730', was added, was there any impact. 'In 1818, Monsieur Bohne wrote from St Petersburg; "My Honored friend, it is considered here that the wine of Mr Cliquot is a nectar . . . I shall be adored".' This appeared in a *Harpers and Queen* advertisement for Revillon, furriers since 1723, and anxious that their image should be imbued with the reflected qualities of Cliquot champagne. It invited the reader to agree with the subjective judgements inferred; it flattered, in addition, by expecting recognition of a particular set of accepted standards. The black fur in the advertisement disappeared into a very dark background, but that was almost unimportant; the glow in the reader, caused by identifying with the 'right values', had been achieved.

Bernstein (1974) maintained that advertising is 'a bastard art in the middle of an inexact science'. The creative art of advertising deserves fairer treatment, and indeed receives it currently, to the extent that some observers are wondering if creativity has become the prime objective and communicating with the customer is lost in the mist permeating so many beautiful, award-winning, but ineffective advertising campaigns.

'An inexact science'? Hardly; even as Bernstein, a guru in the world of advertising made his views known, the scientific theories of promotion were already firmly laid. Their bedrock is in psychology, communication science, epistemology, linguistics and semiotics: the behavioural sciences, social sciences, science and technology married to produce effective persuasive power. 'Inexact' is only excusable in the sense that men and women remain individuals and are, therefore, unpredictable.

Even the inference in an advertisement that the reader, or viewer, or listener, has the potential to become the owner of the desired object can sell related goods. *Performance Car* carried the BF Goodrich tyre advertisement, 'Right now, we've a car like yours in mind.' The photograph below showed a Porsche 962; the text extolled the quality of their tyres with an inset showing a portion of tyre with a broad deep tread. They weren't selling tyres, they were persuading that dreams can come true. Libraries and information centres could take note.

However, promotion using strong connotations can only work if it is the user's connotations that are being brought into play, and that can only come from a real understanding of the background and psychological makeup of the target segment.

Cultural connotations

One cannot free oneself from the impact of one's parents, peer-group attitudes, ability and education: all play their part in building up personality and knowledge and thereby responses to stimuli. To what extent does the subconscious acceptance of cultural influences affect responses to promotional communications?

How much does the success of Fairy Snow owe to the 'existence' of Snow White and connotations of purity (from Snow White) and worker (from the seven dwarfs – or should we say for the sake of political correctness, the seven vertically challenged)? The ancients had it that seven planets circled the sun (Snow White equals purity of strong light) and hence seven, not four, or six, dwarfs. 'Hold it up to the light' has entered the language almost as much as 'Hoovering' for vacuuming or 'Biro' for ballpoint pen.

The style of advertisements, whether print or other media, including web based, can arouse strong associations; the use of Gothic typefaces and a fairytale landscape denote old-established values to the European; 'home-spun' sells in North America; cartoons sell to the Italians, where the theatre of the streets is non-stop.

The notion of 'library' raises responses built over centuries and it would be self-defeating to reiterate them here, but what kind of image should librarians and information professionals be seeking to establish and enhance? The British Library Document Supply Centre promoted a high-tech, super-fast service based on a photograph of the huge volume, two-feet high and six-feet wide, *The Pyramids of Gizeh*. Fascinating in itself, but not particularly successful in catching and holding the attention of the businessmen who are reading the journals where the advertisement had been placed.

Cultures in different places, at different times, will respond differently to a particular symbol, but there are symbols where connotations cross international barriers and centuries and the persuader uses them to pursue his own ends: a red cross, a nurse, a nun, will always evoke a particular set of perceptions. Consumers are very much more aware of semiotics and symbolism in promotion, to the extent that phallic symbols provoke groans of dismissal, yet there is obviously power in advertising, a system that allows, indeed invites, a set of manipulative forces into the private home and the individual's mind. Marcuse says the sale of goods 'has been accompanied by moronization, the perpetuation of toil and the promotion of frustration' (1964).

Should librarians and information professionals join the advertisers and benefit by attracting users through the use of these methods, or should they remain faithful to their ethic of objectivity and present only the unvarnished facts as their message? A difficult choice to make in a society where brand names have passed into common culture to the extent that a brand name can describe a person's personality; Black and Decker man or Volvo man would not be expected to flourish boxes of chocolate at his lady, even if she does love Milk Tray. If they are to succeed in reaching their target markets, librarians and informational professionals need to be aware of why and how subjective and cultural meanings are attributed to goods, how people can and do decode visual and verbal imagery or classify on minimal clues, and how expectations have been aroused that advertising should provide rewards, aesthetic, emotional or intellectual. Umberto Eco (1976) on semiotics, Judith Williamson (1978) on ideology and meaning in advertisements, and Cook (1992) on decoding advertisements are useful and accessible; Bettelheim (1979) on cultural meaning in fairytales will illuminate any study of current advertising.

When we know that Beanz meanz Heinz, that Guinness is good for you, when we have a break, have a Kit-Kat, and even non-linguists can say 'Vorsprung durch Technik', why can't we say that libraries are full of Eastern promise?

Libraries and information centres will only succeed if they leave behind the philosophy of 'take us as you find us' and seek to target their markets effectively through differentiated marketing tuned to the specific needs of particular segments.

References and further reading

Barrett, G. (1995) *Forensic marketing*, McGraw-Hill in association with The Marketing Society.

Bernstein, D. (1974) *Creative advertising*, Longman.

Bettelheim, B. (1979) *The uses of enchantment*, Penguin.

Bickerton, P., Bickerton, M. and Pardesi, U. (1996) *CyberMarketing*, Butterworth-Heinemann/The Chartered Institute of Marketing.

Blackwell, R. D., Miniard, P. W. and Engel, J. F. (2001) *Consumer behaviour*, 9th edn, Harcourt.

Brassington, F. and Pettit, S. (2000) *Principles of marketing*, 2nd edn, Pitman.

Chaffey, D. et al. (2000) *Internet marketing: strategy, theory and practice*, Pearson Education.

Cook, G. (1992) *The discourse of advertising*, Routledge.

Eco, U. (1976) *A theory of semiotics*, Indiana University Press.

Faison, E. W. J. (1980) *Advertising; a behavioural approach for managers*, Wiley.

Haig, M. (2000) *e-pr: the essential guide to public relations on the internet*, Kogan Page.

Hammond, K., Ehrenberg, A. and Goodhardt, G. J. (1996) Market segmentation for competitive brands, *European Journal of Marketing*, **30** (12), 30–44.

Jobber, D. (2001) *Principles and practices of marketing*, 3rd edn, McGraw-Hill.

Kotler, P. (2000) *Marketing management: the millennium edition*, 10th edn, Prentice Hall.

McDonald, M. and Dunbar, I. (1995) *Market segmentation*, Macmillan.

McKean, J. (1999) *Information masters; secrets of the customer race*, John Wiley and Son.

Marcuse, H. (1964) *One dimensional man*, Routledge and Kegan Paul.

Maslow, A. H. (1987) *Motivation and personality*, 3rd edn, Harper and Row.

Mitchell, A. (1983) *Nine American lifestyles: who we are and where are we going*, Macmillan.

Palmer, A. (2001) *Principles of services marketing*, 3rd edn, McGraw-Hill.

Payne, A. and Frow, P. (1999) Developing a segmented service strategy: improving measurement in relationship marketing, *Journal of Marketing Management*, **15** (8), 797–818.

Phipps, R. and Simmons, C. (2001) *Marketing customer interface*, Butterworth-Heinemann/The Chartered Institute of Marketing.

Piirto, R. (1991) *Beyond mind games: the marketing power of psychographics*, American Demographic Books.

Rogers, E. H. (1983) *Diffusion of innovations*, 3rd edn, Macmillan.

Seybold, P. (1999) *Customers.com*, Random House.

Sleight, P. (1997) *Targeting customers: how to use geodemographics and lifestyle data in your business*, NTC Publications.

Statt, D. A. (1997) *Understanding the consumer: a psychological approach*, Macmillan.

Tapp, A. (2001) *Principles of direct and database marketing*, 2nd edn, Pearson.

Wells, W. D. and Gubar, G. (1966) Lifecycle concepts in marketing research, *Journal of Marketing Research*, **3** (4), (November), 355–63.

Williamson, J. (1978) *Decoding advertisements:ideology and meaning in adverts*, Marion Boyars.

Wilson, R. M. S. and Gilligan, C. with Housden, M. (1995) *Strategic marketing management*, Butterworth-Heinemann.

7

MARKETING IN THE DIGITAL AGE

Cyber-driven libraries and information services will be very different organizations as the digital, interactive information environment changes the way in which management and staff relate to each other, to suppliers, to distributors, to users and to clients.

Do traditional marketing concepts and practices work in the digital world? This chapter aims to demonstrate that the answer is 'yes' and that the marketing concepts discussed throughout this book are the foundations for the specific online marketing techniques of the digital environment.

The objectives of this chapter are:

- to explore the potential for new roles for librarians and professionals
- to examine the marketing of libraries and information services in the digital age
- to explore an e-marketing mix for libraries and information centres
- to introduce the concepts of customer relationship management and data mining for libraries and information centres
- to identify sources of help on digital legislation.

New roles for librarians and information professionals

Librarians and information professionals, once dealers in artefacts, in selection, collection, storage and retrieval, are now in a very different service profession. A user-centric strategy must be the lodestone of the mission of every library or information service in the digital age.

Librarians and information professionals will need to welcome new markets and new ways of reaching them and to encompass new products and services. Emphases will change, market segments will be different, affected by macroenvironmental changes. The user will become a much more active participant in the marketing process: online customers or users are not passive, they initiate communication, so librarians and information professionals need to think about creating and delivering marketing messages in new ways. Marketing mixes will focus on the individual client or user to a much greater extent.

From know-what to know-how

Librarians and information professionals can use digital technology to create new products and services, to deliver to existing and new markets and to retain the loyalty of individuals in those markets. The same technology can support effective relationships with internal and external partners via intranets and extranets. Marcum (2001, 102) maintains that it is necessary for library managers to 'seek to build networked levels of expertise, from basic know-what to more advanced know-how, to a comprehensive systems understanding (know-why) to the ultimate self-motivated creativity'.

Librarians and information professionals have the skills to ensure quality delivery in an information world, user-centric in the jargon and people-centred in truth. These expert skills and services will need to be marketed to users who are different from 20 years ago, who have different expectations, who may be willing to shed previous conceptions of libraries and information services or perhaps never had them in the first place. 'Libraries own information. They therefore have an inside track in the Information Age, yet often appear not to realise how to use the opportunity,' according to Hooper (2001, 76). Marcum (2001, 100) also has misgivings; he says that although knowledge management has 'exploded onto the scene with powerful tools to measure, capture, nurture and utilize intellectual capital, [these are] underutilized by most corporations'.

Expanding numbers of service companies present real threats to libraries and information services: search engine services for the world wide web, satellite specialist information channels and a variety of infomediaries are setting up. These infomediaries are not information professionals, but providers of services collating information on goods and services and their prices. The user market perceives that new skills are needed for this new world of communication and this new breed of professionals and companies are cashing in, literally, on this perception. Direct digital access offers a means of bypassing the intermediaries in information seeking for some. The majority of the market is still looking for help but not turning to librarians.

'Commercial search engines have, in many instances, become the first port of call for students – and even lecturers – seeking information, often to the detriment of the quality-assured and refereed content provided within subscription services' (Breaks and MacLeod, 2001, 286). Robert Dwek (2000, 59), Editor of *Marketing Week e-volve*, claimed that Yahoo! 'simply know how to collate and present information on the Web better and faster than anyone else'.

'In higher education, academic staff and students now have access to a vast range of subscription-based networked datasets, and there has been a fundamental shift from reliance on print to reliance on electronic resources as the first resort' (Breaks and MacLeod, 2001, 286). The myriad sources of information available in digital format are crying out for the skills of the information professionals, but how often are they consulted?

In addition, in the commercial sector it is imperative that information professionals are part of the team planning and executing intranet and extranet services for their organizations. Too many companies and departments do not realize that good web pages and integrated business intelligence systems come from collaboration between content providers and organizers and digital communication designers. There is a self-evident synergy in their work and network managers and web managers are increasingly coming from the ranks of librarians and information professionals. Part of their marketing strategy must be to take the initiative and demonstrate their information organization and management skills so that they are always integral to the intranet and extranet operation and the offline dialogue is effective internal marketing.

There is no point in librarians and information managers grumbling that they are the professionals, this is what they are trained for, have always done. Librarians and information professionals need:

- to demonstrate that they are the experts
- to deliver quality service
- to deliver it fast
- to the right people, at the right time
- *and to tell the world what they are doing.*

Benson (1997, 26) identifies eight new roles for librarians in 'a global network environment':

1 as internet access providers
2 as navigators
3 as educators
4 as publishers
5 as intermediaries
6 as information evaluators
7 as information organizers
8 as planners and policymakers.

If the role of marketer is not added, there will be no opportunity to take on the other roles.

Marketing libraries and information centres in the digital world

Marketing processes in the digital world are no different initially: exploring and identifying trends, understanding market needs, presenting appropriate marketing mixes and evaluating throughout. The same marketing concepts are fundamental, whatever, wherever and whenever the scenario.

'The founding culture of the Internet – a culture based on openness, access to information and functionality' (Dwek, 2000, 60) is the type of ethical context in which librarians and information professionals have always operated and should feel at home now.

Adams and Clark (2001) on effective communication on the internet is a good start to the process of familiarization for those who need it. Information professionals will find a synergy with their approach and emphasis on evaluating sources, information-seeking skills and effective communication. They provide a lucid account of the internet, its history and its future: their description of how the internet evolved and their forecasts on how society, government and education will decentralize the world in the future make compelling reading.

In the professional literature, Peter Griffiths (2000, 9) provides an 'avowedly non-technical' introduction to managing both internet and intranet services. The *Neal-Schuman complete internet companion for librarians* by Allen C. Benson (1997), in marked contrast, is full of technical know-how on hardware and software and covers hard-core searching and resource discovery. Neither text mentions marketing, although both are keen on 'customers' and there is much implicit marketing theory included, for example Griffiths (2000, 39) looks usefully at the 'shop window' of the website. Both reflect the activities of many librarians and information professionals, who are genuinely concerned about their users and provide excellent services, which would be even better supported and resourced if they were to pursue a more explicit marketing strategy.

Digital PEST and SWOT

Macro-environmental scanning and a micro-environmental audit, a PEST and SWOT, are the essential foundations to marketing in the electronic environment.

In the public sector, markets for libraries services are changing, user expectations have changed rapidly as increasingly they use remote controls from their armchairs, to shop, send e-mails and control their banking via digital TV. Interactivity is no longer confined to the home personal computer user as digital television viewers respond to news programmes, vote-ins and on-air challenges. Access via digital television is likely to be a more comfortable option than via home computers for many segments of the public libraries market.

Libraries must be seen to be credible information purveyors, accessible in the same ways as banks and shops, part of the everyday fabric of life.

Digital mission

A new mission must be formulated. A mission is not set in stone; it must be revised at regular intervals to drive change as well as to take change into account. This does not mean that digital technology takes priority. Technology in all its guises will affect users, services and staff, and this should be reflected in each successive mission statement, but for each library or information service the emphases will be different and they will change over time.

The key to success in the new digital world is to cultivate customer relations, to turn the client, the user, the customer into a partner, in a mutually beneficial relationship. Exploring opportunities with the electronic media demands resources; senior managers must identify key personnel to engage in the discussions and plan for entering the marketplace.

O'Connor and Galvin (2001, 14) believe that in the internet market 'the benefits of first-mover advantage should not be underestimated' when marketing in the digital age. For some organizations, this undoubtedly would be true, and not only for the large multinational information services. A school library, which embraces information and communication technology ahead of the subject departments, will have a massive advantage when marketing services to staff and pupils, and become a priority for funding in governors' eyes. The revised mission will need to encompass the new needs of a technology-literate user base.

A commercial sector information service might look, as a priority, to enhancing availability and speed of services. The same service may need to expand provision via intranet, and also via extranet and internet for a very much wider set of subscribers with different needs; corresponding care will have to be taken with regard to confidentiality.

A university library may be looking to widening access via off-site terminals to academic electronic services, supported by self-teach tutorials and online help desks, to enhance the information-seeking skills of undergraduates and facilitate the research effectiveness of academic staff and postgraduate students.

Public libraries are looking constantly to be an integral part of the life of the community they serve, to enhance quality of life through education, information and leisure services, so it is probable that their mission will include technology as a facility offered and a medium of delivery. Teaching in the use of digital technology will be one of the priorities when a major aim of the mission is access to information, education and leisure sources for all.

The mission cannot ignore the energy vortex of the digital age. Cannon (2000, 43) says 'Focus, focus, focus. Create a set of goals and objectives for your online presence. Forget about tomorrow; it's over before you know it. Think three years out. Think realistically, but aggressively of where you want to be.'

The mission concept is well established as a successful motivator in all types of organization, but the digital age itself may affect the whole concept of mission in the future. A good mission statement is constructed as a result of consultation and there should be support for its aims as a result. Intranet and extranet availability allows for greater and speedier consultation with internal and external markets and, in theory, should lead to even more effective mission formulation. Menzel (2001, 362) takes a contrary view: 'the organizational imperative – that is to get ahead one must swear allegiance and fealty to the company line – is likely to become blurred and pushed aside in favor of a more open, participative, and even a democratic workplace.' He speculates that it is possible that electronic communication can have negative consequences for group life in an organization and imagines 'a workplace that is less civil and ethical insofar as employees treat each other with less respect and consideration' (369–70).

In this context, librarians and information professionals must treat e-mail communications seriously as part of their marketing strategy. E-mails can be downright harmful in public relation terms, both internal and external. E-mails that range in approach from terse to the point of discourtesy to casual and over familiar, with scant regard for spelling or grammar, are common. Thankfully the use of emoticons or 'smileys' is reducing – the chairman or other important client does not always appreciate a smiley wearing sunglasses! There are still websites, however, that appear to invent more emoticons on a daily basis (Adams and Clark 2001, 78–9).

Horrendous e-mail marketing stories abound, and in even the biggest of companies mistakes are made. For example 'In 1999, AT&T sent out an e-mail to 1,800 customers. And put them all in the CC: field. Nissan sent out an update on its newest sport utility vehicle and did the same thing. Only this time the number was 24,000. One can only assume that there was a Ford employee or two among them' (Sterne and Priore, 2000, 151). It is imperative that user confidentiality is respected and the acceptable practice on some intranets of showing distribution lists should not be taken into the extranet or internet domain.

Policies on the use of intranet, extranet and internet services, including confidentiality and the sending of marketing communications only if permission is given, need to form part of the mission statement.

Digital customers

The real difference between traditional marketing and digital marketing is that the technology supports 'the ability to offer an efficient, customized solution' (Hardaker and Graham, 2001, 231).

Librarians and information professionals need to construct their digital marketing mix in this context, the solution that will have users and clients happy to use services and coming back for more. Users subconsciously seek constant sources of psychological and emotional satisfaction, and want to identify with or become loyal to the providers of that satisfaction. Users want to return, just as they want to belong. In traditional marketing, retailers give them greeters at the doors of supermarkets and join-the-club loyalty cards; in the digital world Beenz, UK, pays online customers with its own beenz global currency; restaurants e-mail regular customers with changes to their menu and save their favourite table for them; credit card companies offer incentives on every web page.

Libraries and information centres must follow suit. Readers and users logging into the system can be addressed by name and encouraged to return by specifically targeted information of interest to them: warned that loan materials are about to expire, new items are in stock, new online services available in their subject area, and new legislation enacted relevant to their range of products.

The internet can open up exciting new market opportunities for library and information services. It creates virtual communities of interest and personal relationships, customers who 'choose to visit you on the Web, they talk about you with others in the newsgroups, and you join in. And you talk to them privately by e-mail. If you do it right, you make good friends with your customers' (Sheth and Sisodia, 2001, 229). Communities of interest can also 'lead to pooling of expertise to the extent that they can out-reach even the biggest of corporations' and 'can be a vehicle of powerful consumerist activism' (Hardaker and Graham, 2001, 110–13).

So who are these digitally enabled customers? Jobber (2001, 198) quotes research from Netpoll, based on segmentation criteria such as age, socioeconomic group, gender and lifestyle, adopted here for librarians and information professionals:

> The *gameboy*, aged fifteen, he accesses the Internet mainly at home and thinks he is net-savvy. He can be used by the school librarian to influence his peers if he is encouraged to take on the role of teacher and demonstrator or mentor to younger pupils. He needs to be brought into the Marketing Committee of the School Library. The capital letters are important, Marketing is somewhat 'cooler' (acceptable) than school library monitor.
>
> The *cyberlad*, aged twenty three, he accesses the Internet at work and at home. Jack the lad, he e-mails smut to his friends and thinks he is an expert on the Net. The public library needs to reach this potential customer, he is the future, as he marries, has children, is influential in the local community. Learning for life from his company's information centre or the public library will only attract him if he

can be persuaded that it will give him greater spending power or image polish, so illustrations, language and motivational factors in web links on his work web base or local sports web pages will need to mirror his self image.

The *net sophisticate*, aged twenty eight, straddles the border between cool and nerd, believes he knows more about the Net than anyone. Sites with stickability, encouraging him to stay, will need to quirk his interest and give plenty of interactive opportunities. Sticky sites which encourage users to stay offer screen savers, demand interactivity from the user, update information constantly, provide quizzes and are sometimes 'pay users' for their visit. Sophisticated he may be, but links to intriguing information sources will always pull him in.

The *cybersec*, aged thirty one, she only accesses the Internet at the office, not really into computers, she has started to use the Net for travel arrangements and is beginning to explore. Information skills can be offered online using access to relevant information sites to retain her interest. Like the cyberlad, she will appreciate self recognition in marketing illustrations and links on sites she is likely to visit will lead her into a variety of useful services from either the company or public library. Education libraries and information centres are likely to attract her as females in this age bracket are often looking to self development.

The *infojunky*, aged forty, married with kids, he or she might be a middle ranking professional, likes feeling in touch through the Internet and also feels, perhaps wrongly, that time spent online is a big benefit in their job. He is likely to use local community information websites and he can be targeted with information which can be relayed to his wife and children.

The goal is to make life easier for the users, eliminating complexity for them. Librarians in the UK are using information and communications technology to engender social inclusion 'to counter rural isolation and give a real fillip to adult education', to give the elderly the opportunity 'to catch up with the latest news and develop their life skills' (Cash for ICT access, 2001, 272). In the USA, Proctor and Gamble's chief information officer is offering customers added value in net-based information. The Pampers Parenting Institute website provides expert parenting information for those who need it, when they need it, and 'that could be the middle of the night in their own country' (Mitchell, 2001, 34).

How digital marketing differs from traditional marketing

The differences between traditional and new media in marketing are due to the interactive nature of digital technology, whether the internet, satellite, digital television or mobile phones (Kiani, 1998). The real difference is in treating the customer as a partner in the provision of services. This goes beyond the understanding of reader or user needs to welcoming input from the user. The user can make a difference in this way to the actual service offered, for example by choosing to have it delivered to suit his convenience, by a particular medium, at a particular time, even at a particular quality level.

Other differences centre on the customized nature of the digital transaction. See Figure 7.1.

The digital marketing mix

E-product

Among the concepts that are driving electronic commerce is that in the Information Age, information itself is the product.

(Hooper, 2001, 76)

Library and information centre products will be in the form of information in digital format, current awareness services, document delivery (with attention to licence issues and copyright), course materials in education sectors and product information in commercial sectors, in addition to user services, via websites, such as access to catalogues and interrogation of borrower data and frequently asked questions pages. For all these digital transactions, language, level and complexity of instructions need to be designed with the users in mind and need to be market tested. This last is too often ignored.

There are new opportunities to be exploited in new markets and products and there is undoubtedly competitive advantage where a library might introduce a service into the community ahead of other potential suppliers: IT training; education or work opportunity support; or online access to national

Traditional Marketing	Digital Marketing
Mass-marketing	Individualized marketing or mass customization
Segmentation	Communities of the like minded
User as a target	User as a partner
Supply users	Users demand
One to many communications	One to one Or many to many communications
Branding	Communication two way
Monologue	Dialogue

Fig. 7.1 *Traditional and digital marketing differences (after Kiani, 1998)*

and local government policies, documents and debate, for example.

The much heralded e-book revolution has become a damp squib and not because e-books cannot be read in the bath. Despite the plethora of information sources on the world wide web, some librarians believe that web availability will not wholly or even substantially reduce the demand for hard-copy documents for some considerable time. In a market where less than 10% of readers want e-books, according to research from Accenture (formerly Andersen Consulting), publishers will not release books for digitization, nor will they invest heavily in doing it for themselves (Hyams, 2001, 280).

Cannon (2000, 11) maintains that marketing the electronic product is little different from marketing any other product:

1 Create a product that meets the needs of the consumer (customer research).
2 Tell the consumer about the product (advertising, PR).
3 Answer the consumer's questions and concerns to close a sale (sales) – for libraries and information centres this would translate to ensure they use the service.
4 Listen to the consumer to ensure the product and the service continues to meet the customer's needs (customer service, sales).

It is this last, 'continues to meet the customer's needs', which librarians and information professionals have largely failed to address, where technology can help them to achieve this aim in the future and ensure success for their services. Cannon (2000) says 'the key to successful marketing on the Internet is to initiate and maintain a conversation with the online consumer that starts well before they decide to purchase a product and continues well after they have paid'. Despite years of outreach programmes, many professionals still find it difficult to make approaches, to support and sustain that sense of individual relationship as far as the reader or user is concerned. Relationship management, discussed later in this chapter, must become a marketing priority for librarians and information professionals.

Websites are products

An effective website, frequently visited and revisited because it is informative, entertaining and continually updated, must be a priority if the library or information centre wishes to engage with the digital world fully. A website is a product, it is also a superb promotion device if done well, and in marketing mix terms, it is definitely 'place', a major channel of access.

The first step is to decide why the library or information centre wants a website. Will it be the service's flagship product internally via an intranet, will it support corporate image and information seekers via an extranet and will it interface with the wide world audience via the internet?

Intranet and extranet

An intranet is the network within an organization that enables access to the information of that organization using the tools of the internet. Web browsers and e-mail provide password-protected information and processes to organization staff only. Internal marketing is crucial to the library and information centre and the internal audience will be as critical as the external, if not more so. The library or information centre's web provision should aim to provide the template for other departments.

An extranet extends the intranet facilities, or part of them, and again is password protected, to external users, clients, customers, suppliers, partners and even sometimes competitors. The major drug companies, for example, are making some of their research work available to other companies in their field. The extranet concept is very much within the philosophy of openness discussed earlier and not merely an order progress checking device, although supplier and customer benefit from transaction-tracking access. Information professionals will need to monitor the information available to extranet subscribers most carefully since intellectual capital in the commercial sector has a price. To balance what can be made accessible with what must remain confidential is a complex, ever changing challenge.

Internet

The information purveyors, librarians and information professionals, must be absolutely professional when putting their wares on the internet. The website needs to combine an existing marketing mix with a dot.com marketing paradigm to reach intranet, extranet and internet users.

The site has to target appropriate segments, deliver relevant content, solicit responses, provide tailor-made solutions and encourage users to return. It needs to attract users, engage their interest, encourage participation, response and feedback, in order to build user profiles and retain their loyalty. The virtual user needs to be moved from hit only to visitor. Establishing a dialogue is vital, with welcome features such as a visitors' book. The site needs to appear relevant to users, to pull visitors in and persuade them to stay. A good website will offer services: frequently asked questions is a favourite. It can be used to inform, to persuade, to entertain and to advocate (Adams and Clark, 2001).

Customer value is the key to content, aimed at and packaged for specific market segments. Customer orientation focuses on user need, and users will vary from the super-sophisticated to first-time and scared. Targeting specific segments, addressing users directly and signposting them to 'their' links, via directions to their pages, encouraging interactivity, will keep them coming back. The development of specialized communities and online discussion groups in which library and information staff play a full part will also encourage loyalty and return visits. Knowledge-sharing systems, document sharing and organization templates for document preparation processes, news updates and legislation updates will be useful. The provision of online ordering facilities for reports, statistics, reservations etc., delivered online or offline, will be valued.

The library or information service will be able to turn to colleagues and departments in their organization for help in technical construction, but good web design is essential. Senior management must face up to the need for appropriate resources from the very early stages and provide for the posts of web manager and web designer.

The library or information centre may have to live with corporate branding. Where an organization is operating a portal system, a gateway to a variety of sites linked to the portal, standard design features are usual which may cramp marketing house-style options for the library or information service, but *corporate image*, discussed in Chapter 9, is crucial in marketing. That said, ownership of the web pages, if not site, should be clearly that of the library or information centre. It must be seen as a website that has credibility. It needs to stress the identity and reputation of the library or information centre and give online and offline contact details.

Treating the website as a product or service will help to confirm the need for budgets and resources at a level equivalent to other services offered. There is a real danger, even today in large organizations, that budgets are not realistic. Gone are the days when the web presence was left in the hands of the first volunteer interested in the internet, but because it is perceived as a cheap medium, the level of resources needed is not forthcoming. 'The average product life cycle of a website is just months – aim to live long and prosper,' says Gabay (2000, 96). But prosperity comes at a price, and users will only return if the site offers what they want: instant satisfaction, helpful links, good navigation features and currency. That takes time, it takes expertise and it takes resources.

E-place

Technology, via CD-ROM, online bibliographic databases and access to the internet, is the norm; complementing this provision with staff development and user education is altering the traditional face of the library or information centre everywhere.

Libraries have offered electronic interfaces via on-street, or campus-wide, information points for years and they have been important in extending the services of the institutions offering them. The greatest weakness of these services in the users' eyes has been their lack of interactivity; that situation is changing as extranet and internet capability is added to some of them.

Enabling the user to access the library or information centre from the workspace, student desk or home is a much wider undertaking.

Just as in the physical environment, the virtual environment must reflect the identity and image of the service. It is the very public face of the service. The physical library or information centre will be accessible to relatively small numbers in comparison with those who are entering its virtual portals. The website should be treated as representative of the library or information centre, in the way that a sales representative would be trained, appraised and progress evaluated. Feedback on internet, intranet and extranet presence should be actively sought and acted upon. Pages under construction should be kept away from the website until they are ready for public consumption: a building site would not allow public access until the building was ready.

Reciprocal links will enhance image as well as making the site more useful and 'sticky'. Disclaimers may be needed to indicate the library or information centre is not responsible for the validity of information in such links. The linked sites need to be checked regularly and if they are not performing, cut the link: no matter how many disclaimers, the user will blame the library or information centre for a poor result and wasted time and energy. Synergy with hyperlinks is even more important in the digital marketing context as the users are self-selecting segments, with identical or very similar characteristics, and they will be benchmarking the linked services against that of the library or information service.

An operational plan is needed: what are the objectives; who are the target audiences on internet, intranet and extranet; who will manage the functions of information provision and design? The service needs to pay for professional design and maintenance, just as the fabric of a building is resourced. If there is hollow laughter at the thought, remind senior management of health and safety regulations – the health and survival of the service is at risk if the website is failing demonstrably.

A decision on house style will have to be made re intranet, extranet and intranet web pages when corporate conformity is not required. It might be tempting to think that language and style might be different for each audience, but it raises the question of why the service is presenting three separate images for the users who come in via all routes?

Easy access via a recognizable and memorable domain name will generate traffic to the site. 'What's in a name' is even more important here. The URL (Uniform Resource Locator) of the library or information centre's site or particular pages must be given in online and offline publications even when the site or pages lie within an organization website; otherwise there is a risk that intending users will click off.

Website construction

Supplying detailed information on the construction of websites is not a purpose of this text. There are very many professional services on website construction available, many, obviously, via the web, providing advice on such matters as banner advertising and metadata (see below). Manuals are published daily; one of the most useful, with a reader-friendly text, is that of Adams and Clark (2001) who also include a WebBuilder CD-ROM on constructing websites.

Adams and Clark (2001, 223) say 'think of metaphors': the website is the supermarket, perhaps with goods sorted by category shoppers need; there is a check-out facility and a customer service department. Think of the express till: one click should take the user back to the home page.

Librarians and information professionals need to travel through this virtual place at regular intervals, to check for jargon and ambiguity in links, to listen to what users are saying, to try to put themselves in the place of the user.

The best-organized sites are clear and simple to use. The user wants an easy progress through the website: information on screen-sized pages, links, buttons and menu areas highlighted all help. Research shows that a substantial number of users never scroll down, so that information or links are lost to them. Users want to find things quickly: good signposting and hyperlinks that allow a variety of routes to the required information help. Navigation buttons in the same place help too. Users are not willing to drill down through page after page: three tends to be maximum before click off. Clean the site and individual pages regularly of out-of-date, extraneous information and add news or different items. Sites that are visually appealing, but complicated to navigate or time consuming to download pages, will be rejected.

Metadata

User capture, the ability to attract users is vital. Using appropriate metadata, keywords in the text of pages, to ensure that search engines list the library or information service site and capture the user is one method.

Established web services such as search engines publish helpful guides to using metadata and search engine know-how on being included in the top 20 sites listed in response to searches; on how to include keywords on every page to enhance position in listings; and how to avoid spamming, the deliberate repetition of keywords that will be screened out anyway by the search engine robot or spider crawlers. It is possible to pack in exciting high usage search terms. Kerr (1999, 40) uses *Titanic*, sex and football to demonstrate how apparently easy it could be to achieve hit ratings, but warns: 'Do not do it.' It will alienate potential users and these days will probably result in the site being penalized by search engines.

In the competitive world of user capture, it is important to be credible and retain integrity.

E-promotion

There will be few libraries and information centres currently able to offer sub-scriber satellite channels in the fashion of some of the world's famous football clubs. Most will depend for the foreseeable future on the website as a marketing tool.

The website, when the purpose is promotion, becomes a shop window. Information on the library or information centre will be paramount, although brochureware should be avoided. Brochureware is merely the digitizing of existing promotional publications. It may appear to be an easy and speedy option, but it is best avoided since it ignores the nature of web user segments and is infuriating to the users who request further information offline and are presented yet again with the same information.

Design obviously plays a part in promoting the website and, even more importantly, it promotes the image of the library or information service. Again, it should not be necessary to say, but this is not a job in their spare time for the member of staff keen on computers. Manage and resource the website as you would any other project and there is a better chance of success.

The library and information centre website message needs to be reinforced everywhere; offline promotion of the web address is as important as online: the URL must be on every piece of stationery, every delivery van, every inter-nal and external noticeboard, every company or authority newsletter, on coasters in the coffee lounge and, of course, on every e-mail.

E-public relations

The internet, extranet and intranet offer endless opportunities for dialogue. How the communications are handled is very much at the heart of market-ing communication strategy.

The mission can be expounded directly to the market. Other messages can be relayed immediately, without the danger of intermediaries changing, dis-torting or delaying the message. Care needs to be exercised here: a too rapid response to a market situation may lead to potential misinformation or state-ments that, with hindsight, could have been communicated at a different level of information or with a different approach in public relation terms.

Interaction with users should be sought only if it can be maintained. Dialogue with users is an attractive marketing desirable, but it should be invited only when the library or information centre can afford the interactivity demand on staff.

The effect, on both internal and external audiences, of poorly written, inappropriate approaches and responses must be considered. For example, it is usually considered desirable for e-mail addresses of individual staff to be publicized on a website, but staff need to be fully aware of their role and responsibilities for responses. Policies on who has responsibility to speak on behalf of the library or information centre, for example, must be decided at the strategic level, as every employee with access to e-mail becomes a potential spokesperson.

E-price

Cost to the user includes time spent at the site. Often that will have a cash price attached too, which users are ever more aware of. User time, therefore, in all senses is an expensive commodity. The more easily users can access the library or information centre site and find what they want quickly, the more likely they are to be in a relaxed mode and the more likely they will stay and then return, service marketing objectives achieved.

Users are self-electing: they have chosen to visit the site, just as they choose to watch a television programme, but time spent at a site must be of value to the user. They are less critical of television viewing, in that they use their viewing time for other activities too.

Users live in an exciting visual world and many media rely on instant response to image to promote their message: broadcast and print media advertisements, billboard messages, television commercials that impinge on the subconscious even in a video recording in fast-forward mode. The library and information service has to decide in the image v. information dilemma. Pretty images and opening sequences at the expense of a clean, professional-looking site should not be the decision arrived at. Crucial to decisions on what a home page should look like is that a page without text will not be picked up by the search engines, reducing the chances of user capture. More important to the user, if a home page contains solid information there has been no waiting cost while the images scroll past.

Shopping for information

E-commerce is expanding fast as businesses are protected by legislation and consumers gain confidence in digital media. Television and satellite shopping, terrestrial and analogue, have broken initial resistance barriers and the move to digital appears to be seamless for the existing home shopper. Information centres intending to levy charges for access may find that their focus needs to be on levels of charging for different segments of their markets, *differential pricing*, rather than questioning whether they will alienate users by charging.

Public libraries will need to offer their publications and other products for sale via online charging and online credit facilities, which are easily set up with professional help. Equally, academic libraries offering offprints from bibliographic databases, for example, will need to negotiate with campus provision of student and staff credit schemes. The British Library is one of the leading partners in the world's first entirely e-commerce-enabled digital heritage image library. Inaugurated in Spring 2001, it makes available images from the collections of libraries, museums, galleries and institutions, at a price.

Users are now used to digital competition and shop for the best deal from banks and product retailers via interactive services. Their perception will be that they can shop for information too and they may surf the internet for 'the best deal', without any realization that their criteria in searching could be flawed, affected by factors such as appearance or speed of response. The price paid could be wrong information.

Customer relationship management

The electronic 'Ps' (see Chapter 4) of the marketing mix are based on the familiar marketing formula. E-mail marketing, discussed in Chapter 5, also follows the traditional format. Librarians and information professionals must begin to add another dimension to their marketing portfolio in the digital age: relationship marketing and, in particular, customer relationship management (CRM).

The theories are the latest to exercise marketers. The ability to have a complete customer profile, at the touch of a button while the customer transaction is taking place, is comparatively recent. The opportunities to enhance the customer experience, market other services and retain customer loyalty are immense if handled well. The key idea in the new digital world is to cultivate customer relations, to turn the client, the user, the customer into a partner, in a mutually beneficial relationship. Relationship marketing and customer relations management are the keys to success.

Relationship marketing is about establishing, maintaining and enhancing contacts with users, with suppliers and with distributors. Customer relationship management is concerned with current users and how to retain them: making the user feel welcome, learning as much as possible about the user, identifying all the characteristics discussed in segmentation, plus opinion, attitude and behaviour where possible, so that the product and service offering can be enhanced to appear a tailor-made, personalized service. Satisfied users and readers, comfortable in their relationships with the library or information centre, will remain loyal and they will become a sales force themselves, attracting colleagues, family members and other students to the services. 'Customer relationship management is a holistic process of identifying, attracting, differentiating, and retaining customers,' say Strauss and Frost (2001, 284) in their work on e-marketing. They describe it as 'participatory marketing, a shared community where everyone involved benefits from each other in an environment of mutual gain' (2001, 325).

Internet marketing research repeatedly shows that companies which score highly in customer service satisfaction (answering questions, solving problems and responding to complaints quickly) are always more successful than competitors. Librarians and information professionals might take note of research from the Round consultancy in March 2000 which ranked car parts replacement company, Kwik-Fit, top for excellence in its customer relationship programme (Donald, 2000, 90); Amazon.com came second. Approximately 5500 people are called every day within 72 hours of a visit to a Kwik-Fit centre and canvassed on their views of the service they received. Peter Holmes, Kwik-Fit Group Director of Marketing, is adamant about their 'uncompromising customer service ethos'. Holmes says, 'to retain loyalty you have to work very hard. Nobody takes any pleasure in having parts of their cars replaced – it's a distress purchase – so we try our hardest to make the experience as pleasurable as possible so that they will hopefully come back in the future.'

'Make the experience as pleasurable as possible': the library or information centre needs market research to find out what would help the user to feel happier. This could be via online focus groups or surveys, suggestions boxes on the website or in-house. Listening to the user will always help build a relationship. Communicating on the progress of enquiries, new services relevant to that user, information sources newly published in their area, will make a user feel valued by the library or information centre. Creating satisfaction, building trust, developing an ongoing relationship, knowing the individual user, not just understanding segment needs, is now possible as a result of digital technology.

People are wary of being 'databased', but capturing user, client and customer data is essential. A customer relationship strategy aims to identify:

- what users want
- what to say to them
- when to say it
- what medium to use
- how to gain their trust
- how to retain their loyalty.

Once a user has experienced a good service situation then custom and habit will lead to the likelihood of staying with the initial service provider. It is worth reminding purse holders that it is much more cost effective to hold on to existing users than to expend resources on campaigns seeking new markets, and that resources to cultivate the relationship with existing users are vital.

Digital technology can effectively enhance communications with users, between staff, information staff and others in the organization, and with suppliers and distributors. Control can be exercised, via tracking for example, to add further dimensions to a service and should be thought of as adding to a quality service and delivery, not merely as a performance measure. Value is added to the transaction by the ability to inform, in real time, on the progress of information gathering, document preparation, document delivery or request handling, for example.

The librarian or information professional may argue that relationships with users have always been important; what the digital age is offering is an opportunity to make them easier, faster and more effective from the individual user point of view.

Implicit in customer relationship management is the differentiated marketing customer focus vital in the digital world. Relationships with customers, users and clients must be nurtured. The digital world offers real opportunity for coming closer to the user and a better understanding of user needs. Knowledge of the user base, markets segmented to the level of the individual with the help of digital technology, opportunities for capturing user data via digital technology, data mining potential for forecasting and planning are all possible. The user can be integrated into information product and service design and service delivery decisions, so that the relationship really is mutually beneficial.

Permission-based marketing

Permission-based marketing is integral, as well as being a legal requirement, in customer relationship marketing management. The user has to agree that he or she can be approached and is happy to be sent marketing communications. Registration of new members to a service can include, online or offline, a statement for the reader or user to sign. Existing users can be approached, via online or direct mail, to 'renew their service contract'; they can be offered new membership 'cards' or 'rights' that will enable the collection of more information and relevant permissions.

Academic libraries already have a captive community in their staff and students, but need to consider their business and specialist users. Information centres in large organizations or companies may be allowed restricted access to the organization personnel records and should certainly ask for details of new members of staff so that they can be contacted. Public libraries can depend for initial contacts on public domain information but need to turn this into user acceptance before further personal approaches.

Seth Godin's *Permission marketing* (1999) is hailed as the 'bible' in this area of digital marketing. Godin, Vice President Direct Marketing at Yahoo! says harassing best customers is harmful (2000, 38): they need to agree to receive communications such as a newsletter or information on new products, otherwise they switch off from the message and from the organization.

Libraries and information centres should be wary of the use of 'cookies' as they are disliked by web users and open to abuse. Once a site has been visited, cookies can be placed on personal computer desktops by that website. Only an identification number should be contained in a cookie and the host of the website should keep other details in a database to prevent misuse. Cookies have great potential for contacting users of the website again and can be used to track user behaviour so that, with a good webmaster, a user can be contacted with personalized content of value to them. However, because users suspect that their details are being spread by cookies, there is great antagonism towards them, and it is probably safer for libraries and information centres to tread warily as providers or users.

Data mining

Data mining is the new technique aiming at the discovery of patterns of valuable information within large data repositories. It aims at the discovery of 'enterprise [organization] knowledge from historical data and combines historic enterprise knowledge with current conditions and goals' (Delmater and Hancock, 2001, Chapter 2). Information retrieval and analysis are at the heart of data mining, but the big difference for librarians and information professionals is that data mining discovers *interrelationships* worthy of further investigation, 'hot spots' in the data features. Companies are mining their massive databanks, or data warehouses, to investigate clusters of market categories or segments and classifying data, both quantitative and qualitative, as it arrives every day, sometimes via direct mail responses, loyalty cards and the like.

Data mining supports organizations to use data in the management of customer relationships: customer behaviour patterns, unsuspected previously, will show up in the comprehensive correlation techniques of data mining. Data mining is predictive in detecting patterns and trends that could lead to new goals for the organization and different patterns of behaviour in user contact.

The tools of data mining are discussed by Delmater and Hancock (2001, Chapter 2) in a user-friendly guide that ranges through business intelligence systems and information access control to knowledge discovery in databases, to data warehouses, the comprehensive data repository of an organization and data marts, which focus on a specific organization function. 'As computer generation of data outstrips human ability to assimilate data, organizations become "data rich and information poor" . . . high-end analytical capabilities including the exploitation of data patterns for applications involving identification and prediction . . . are called data mining' (Delmater and Hancock, 2001, 4).

Data rich and information poor

Is it possible that this refers to libraries and information centres in relation to their users and clients? How much use is made of reader registration detail, loan patterns, information request behaviour? Valuable resources could be saved, used more effectively, when trends in behaviour are analysed. Trend analysis would prevent staff on standby at times when services are underused, stock replacement in areas no longer heavily used, paying for individual transactions with an outside supplier over and over again, when a subscription or contract would provide better rates and possibly a better relationship and service from the supplier. User behaviour may throw up patterns that identify a need for a change in service offering: specialist help available at particular times of the day, week, month or year. An analysis of data from a frequently asked questions web page may show particular market segment usage, which would imply potential in seeking market research information on their needs.

Mark Schiff, Director of Data Warehousing Strategy at the US company Current Analysis, says it is important to remember that 'just because two events seem to have a high correlation, does not necessarily mean that there is a direct cause-and-effect relationship. For example, there is a high correlation between the number of churches in a town and the number of crimes committed. This does not mean that church-going people are robbing collection plates or that criminals are religious – both events correlate with population' (Faragher, 2000, 48).

Market research can be very much more easily managed in the digital world, although special attention must be paid to permission marketing, since it is imperative that the user is happy to agree to his or her personal information being used for marketing purposes including research responses. Data capture has a whole raft of legislation and ethical considerations to be adhered to for successful relationships to be built.

Interactive marketing, intelligent marketing information systems, customer relationship marketing and data mining all have supporting software and companies offering their services. Add an extranet and intranet service platform as a medium for supplier relation management, and successful marketing strategy is assured.

The more successful customer relationships are, the more sound the future development of the library or information centre will be.

Digital legislation

ACL International, the Association of Commercial Lawyers, is a good source of information and advice in the minefield of digital legislation. Librarians and information professionals must pay attention to: data protection, outsourcing agreements, intellectual property, cyberfraud, computer misuse, domain name disputes, web advertising issues, e-mail and internet access policies in the workplace, and online content provider issues, including defamation.

Librarians and information professionals are as aware as data controllers that the use of lists from published directories, for example, may infringe copyright, but there are other traps for the unwary. For instance 'unfair and unlawful' processing practices, such as 'indirect disclosure' may occur when lists of users from another source enable the user responding to be identified with a number of characteristics that the user had not intended the 'new' marketer to know. The journal *Data Protection and Privacy Practice* is well worth subscribing to. Its editor points to the three relevant core concepts: legislation, regulation and codes of practice (Pounder, 2000, 128). Librarians and information professionals in digital marketing need to:

- abide by data protection legislation (Data Protection Act 1998 in the UK)
- seek the consent of the data subject (the user and permission marketing)
- present clear and obvious advice on how information might be used and opt-out methods offered.

Costs

There is an argument that marketing costs can be reduced as a result of digital technology: reduction is measured against such factors as reductions in staffing and against the cost of hard-copy marketing communications. This is a fallacy: substantial costs are involved and not just because of the technology. Libraries and information services have both set-up and ongoing maintenance costs in hardware and software to contend with, as any organization would, but there will be a major escalation in cost, rather than reduction, as user relationship management techniques develop and there is greater interaction inclusive of human resource (Barney, 2002, 155). Customer service improvement lies in the customer's ability to be an active participant in the process, amending, making decisions, asking for and receiving feedback. This enhances service delivery to an unprecedented degree. Where service improvement does not lie is in the mere provision of a website that may be no more than brochureware, the provision of a duplicate copy of existing marketing materials on a website.

Dialogue between the user and the service is essential and it will further improve the user experience if the user is able to join with others in a community dialogue on the library or information centre website. Users have self-selected in using the technology format and will be a ready target for relevant marketing communications.

Stickiness

Creating stickiness is the main goal of many digital providers: webmasters design sticky websites that encourage the user or browser to stay and television programmers use devices to keep the viewers from their kettles or changing channels.

> Library management should find ways to create 'stickiness' through encouraging a sense of ownership of the library by its customers, to create systems that require the customers to leave part of themselves behind . . . if one can exploit technology to personalise the library service in response to that interaction the customer will develop a sense of ownership and belonging that can only enhance the stature and the service of the library concerned. (Hooper, 2001, 76)

The advice holds good for all library and information centres, from the smallest school or branch library to the largest of multinational business corporation information services.

References and further reading

Adams, T. and Clark, N. (2001) *The internet: effective online communication*, Harcourt College.

Barnes, H. B. (2001) *Secrets of customer relationship management*, McGraw-Hill.

Barney, J. B. (2002) *Gaining and sustaining competitive advantage*, Prentice Hall.

Benson, A. C. (1997) *Neal-Schuman complete internet companion for librarians*, Neal-Schuman.

Breaks, M. and MacLeod, R. (2001) Joining up the academic information landscape, *Library Association Record*, **103** (5), 286–9.

Cannon, J. (2000) *Make your website work for you*, McGraw-Hill.

Cash for ICT access waves hello (2001) *Library Association Record*, **103** (5), 272.

Chaffey, D. et al. (2000) *Internet marketing: strategy, implementation and practice*, Financial Times/Prentice Hall.

Christopher, M., Payne, A. and Ballantyne, D. (2001) *Relationship marketing*, 2nd edn, Butterworth-Heinemann.

Delmater, R. and Hancock, M. (2001) *Data mining explained: a manager's guide to customer-centric business intelligence*, Digital Press.

Donald, H. (2000) Lessons in netiquette, *Marketing Means Business for the CEO*, (Spring), 90–5.

Dwek, R. (2000) Web marketing round-up, *Marketing Means Business for the CEO*, (Spring), 58–61.

Faragher, J. (2000) Digging deeper into data, *Information Age*, (July), 48.

Gabay, J. J. (2000) *Successful cyberm@rketing in a week*, Hodder and Stoughton/Institute of Management.

Godin, S. (1999) *Permission marketing*, Simon and Schuster.

Godin, S. (2000) Reap what you sow!, *Marketing Means Business for the CEO*, (Spring), 36–41.

Griffiths, P. (2000) *Managing your internet and intranet services: the information and library professional's guide to strategy*, Library Association Publishing.

Hardaker. G. and Graham, G. (2001) *Wired marketing: energizing business for e-commerce*, John Wiley and Sons.

Hooper, T. (2001) Management issues for the virtual library, *The Electronic Library*, **19** (2), 71–7.

Hyams, E. (2001) Bringing e-books to journal, *Library Association Record*, **103** (5), 280–1.

Jobber, D. (2001) *Principles and practice of marketing*, 3rd edn, McGraw-Hill.

Kerr, M. (1999) *How to promote your website effectively*, Aslib/Information Management International.

Kiani, G. (1998) Marketing opportunities in the digital world, *Internet Research: Electronic Networking Applications and Policy*, **8** (2), 185–94.

Marcum, J. W. (2001) From information center to discovery system: next step for libraries?, *The Journal of Academic Librarianship*, **27** (2), 97–106.

Menzel, D. C. (2001) Issues and challenges facing public managers. In Sheth, J., Eshghi, A. and Krishnan, B. C. (eds), *Internet marketing*, Harcourt College.

Mitchell, A. (2001) Virtual reinvention, *Marketing Business*, (July/August), 34.

O'Connor, J. and Galvin, E. (2001) *Marketing in the digital age*, 2nd edn, Financial Times/Prentice Hall.

Pounder, C. (2000) Minding data, *Marketing Means Business for the CEO*, (Spring), 123–8.

Sheth, J. N., Eshghi, A. and Krishnan, B. C. (2001) *Internet marketing*, Harcourt College.

Sheth, J. N. and Sisodia, R. S. (2001) Feeling the heat, part 2: Information technology, creative management boost marketing productivity. In Sheth, J. N, Eshghi, A. and Krishnan, B. C. (eds), *Internet marketing*, Harcourt College.

Sterne, J. and Priore, A. (2000) *Email marketing*, John Wiley.

Strauss, J. and Frost, R. (2001) *E-marketing*, 2nd edn, Prentice Hall.

8

MARKETING RESEARCH AND MARKET RESEARCH

Marketing research is active and aim-oriented; it draws on statistics, psychology, sociology and anthropology. Marketing research looks at marketing mixes, pricing research, the effectiveness of advertising and investigates the whole of marketing communication.

Market research is a subset of marketing research. It aims at identifying, measuring and testing your markets, so that services and products can be more effectively targeted.

In practice, librarians and information professionals will find that the terms 'marketing research' and 'market research' are used virtually interchangeably, although the terms are used correctly in context in what follows here.

The objectives of this chapter are:

- to examine marketing research and market research with relevance to libraries and to information centres and services
- to identify what the librarian and information professional needs to know
- to explore a variety of research methods that librarians and information professionals can use
- to argue the cost-effectiveness of employing market research professionals
- to identify the elements necessary in the design of market research.

- What do you need to know?
- Why do you need to know?
- By when do you need to know?
- How do you aim to find out?

Whatever kind of library or information service is operating, the service involves the collection, collation, classification and dissemination of information. The paradox is that there is still no substantial culture of market research, information gathering, evaluation and publication regarding users in the information world. Where reports of research are made they are seized with eagerness. The ease of electronic publishing, however, does not help the research process itself. Thorough grounding of research, results and credibility are paramount before publication. Where communication via the web can help is in decisions on the research process, in the sharing and discussion of methods used, in advice from colleagues who have investigated their markets or are curious about behaviour patterns in similar libraries or information centre situations. The use of the internet, via e-mail and websites for customer responses, is, as one would expect, a growing area of market research when specific segments are investigated.

We may question why it is essential that librarians and information professionals should value marketing research when Piercy (1992, 191) tells us: 'on the things that matter most, we cannot reduce uncertainty to zero or anything like it'. Piercy suggests that while we must consider the need for market research and information, we must also remember that making decisions can never be wholly scientific; that multiple goals, the impossibility of isolating one decision from a plethora of others, and the individualistic approaches of managers, are among the things that 'get in the way' of the scientific approach.

Understanding marketing research

Why then must librarians and information professionals understand marketing research, insist that it be carried out and further, that it be conducted professionally, with all the serious implications that has for timing and funding? Marketing research is essential to effective strategic planning and implementation and its consideration needs to be a continual process for most libraries and information services in the present complex and constantly changing world. The information generated must be put to effective use in forecasting, planning, instructing and illuminating the whole management decision-making process.

Marketing research can also be used as a promotional tool. The planning, implementation, analysis and results can all be used to draw attention to a service. Marketing research activities can highlight an intention to improve services: 'How can we serve you better?' is a fine message to clients and users. Marketing research provides evidence to senior management that there are plans for effectively improving performance and can motivate staff by demonstrating a willingness and ability to listen and to change. Negative findings might be disappointing, but should engender further investigation as to why they are so, thus demonstrating an image of an organization that cares. Positive findings can be trumpeted widely, but it is important not to appear complacent and even more important not to be complacent as a result.

The investigation of current users and client bases as well as potential users and markets, plus the evaluation of current services and products, are essential to the ongoing well-being of the library and information service. Quantitative and qualitative research are needed: quantitative research seeks to measure markets' behaviours, while qualitative research seeks to explore those behaviours and motivations through psychosociological and psychoanalytic techniques with both groups and individuals.

Too many services cannot identify and describe the service users. A complete profile is needed to compare with the actual population of potential users. Pools of non-users who might considerably affect the well-being of a service either through influence, size or future potential as users can be targeted. A profile of by whom and how a service is being used will identify under-used services where the characteristics of a group would suggest a need for the service. Further research will identify why the service is not attracting such users.

In-depth investigations, using appropriate methodology, will provide substantial data for strategic planning and marketing, and will ensure more effective use of resources. General surveys of overall rates of satisfaction with a service will not provide the full picture needed for marketing purposes. Such general data might provide a line manager or committee with a promotional statistic but little more, and these data are expensive to collect for such a small return in value. Data mining can provide more useful, sometimes potentially exciting, illumination in terms of service provision, use and exploitation in comparison.

Corporate executives and senior management prefer reports that are short, clear and simply expressed. An understanding of how data has been collected will enable the librarian and information professional to evaluate the findings more readily and report conclusions with confidence. Addressed to information managers, *Managing information for research* (Orna with Stevens, 1997) is about academic research. It is recommended here because of its straightforward approach to planning the information products of research and presentation design. They say (18–19): 'We are asking ourselves questions and using the answers to design what we are looking for; we are gathering information in the outside world that will enable us to discover what we seek; we are managing the information we gather so that it yields us the maximum help; we are transforming information into knowledge and knowledge back into information.'

Marketing opportunities from research

Marketing opportunities arise all the time out of knowledge of the community in which the service operates. A millennium population boom in one area of Spain is causing difficulties in the provision of pre-school education places. The public library, good at marketing research, continually scanning the environment, experimenting with marketing activities, identified the gap in education provision, saw the marketing opportunity and now provides activities for babies as young as three months. Older siblings as well as their parents are much more aware of other services as a result and the use of other services is growing too.

The European-Commission-funded project 'The public and the library' (Asta and Federighi, 2000) used a variety of methods to research markets, including people who could not read or write. Methods included case study, survey, questionnaire and experiment. One such study, set up by the public library of Isolotto, Florence, put an information and loan centre in the job centre, the Informalavoro, and in the Public Registry Office. Leaflets were distributed, with a short slogan 'Cercavi me?' (Were you looking for me?), in cafés, at hairdressers and under windscreen wipers. Users were interviewed and surveyed by questionnaire. Results were valuable in planning future collaborative efforts between public departments and the library and the university and, even more so, in illuminating the real needs of many sectors of the public library's community: immigrants, refugees, peasants, the unemployed and old people with low incomes.

What do they know?

How many librarians or information professionals know what their users and clients, their customers, know about their services? Simple facts such as opening hours or service availability can make a huge difference to service use when well publicized, but how often is the effectiveness of the publicity checked?

Tuning service availability to market need is part of the marketing mix. Starting with such fundamentals as 'What do they know?' will often provide startling results and will influence the marketing mix. How many departments in companies and other organizations pay for regular and expensive packaged statistics or trend bulletins when the information is already there in their own in-house information service? How many chief executives or communication directors are aware of the information service staff's specific skills in selecting, prime, up-to-date, verifiable sources ahead of need when a crisis is looming? How many banks would direct start-up businesses to their nearest public and academic libraries for product, market and competition information?

Operational planning and marketing research

The organization's operational plan is significantly strengthened by the inclusion of systematic evaluation of implemented strategies and tactics. There needs to be a recognized, structured information flow and pattern of responses to research findings. The regular monitoring of service use, for example, will highlight unexpected patterns or identify trends that may need further investigation, as well as providing fundamental information on the information service, the way services are used and rates of satisfaction with those services. Research that identifies regular peaking of enquiries may very well show up a need to check how many unsatisfied enquirers there are because of heavy traffic on telephone or fax lines and take steps to remedy this. The university library that identifies growing numbers of missing serial issues may need to look at loan policies on periodicals, availability of photocopiers, or tutors' reading lists, etc.

The huge international company Corning, with 29,000 employees worldwide, initiated an Electronic Information Exchange Intelligence System as early as 1989, which, operating through an e-mail system, acts as an information switchbox to relay customer information to key elements of the organization. Corning's information system was hailed as a 'vitally important and effective tool for the corporation' in its marketing and total quality success (Fuld, 1992).

Planning marketing research

A library or information service that is part of a large organization with an in-house marketing research function has the same need as the service that must go to an outside company. It must communicate clearly:

- why information is needed
- what kind of information is needed
- how the data can usefully be presented
- to whom
- by when.

Initial research may be needed in early stages to help to define a problem more clearly.

Kotler (2000, 103) defines marketing research as 'the systemic design, collection, analysis and reporting of data and findings relevant to a specific marketing situation'. Librarians and information professionals need to have a broad foundation of knowledge on research techniques to allow them to control effectively the planning and subsequent interpretation of research in their required market situation. Otherwise there is a real danger that inappropriate information is collected, or that findings are interpreted incorrectly. There are numerous and excellent tomes on research methodology that the librarian and information professional can have great satisfaction in perusing. It is essential that as a result they do not decide to conduct all their market research themselves, for that way lies ruination. Desk research, using secondary data, is largely excluded from this warning, since who would be better than the information professional at identifying and using these sources of intelligence competently; nevertheless the analysis of trends and tendencies calls for care and not a little statistical knowledge.

Research can be continuous or *ad hoc*. The objectives of the librarian or information professional in mounting the research will need to be considered in conjunction with costs and value, as always. Cost will always be an influential factor in the decision-making process, but the real cost will often lie in not carrying out the research and making expensive mistakes as a result. Fairly simple needs may be answered by omnibus surveys, that is, a method of having questions inserted into general (hence omnibus) surveys operated regularly by research companies across large numbers of the population. This is comparatively cheap, but unlikely to prove an effective form of information gathering where a specific library or information service is involved.

Techniques of market research have evolved from elementary surveys, based on observation, in the early years of this century, to the sophisticated multidimensional, econometric and attitude models supported by computer software of today.

173

Market research plan

The design of the market research process, the market research plan, remains constant:

- Define the problem.
- Define objectives.
- Identify resources of information.
- Collect secondary data.
- Design research instrument.
- Construct samples of population.
- Collect primary data.
- Analyse data.
- Present findings.

Chisnall (1997, 36) gives a five-stage process model: research brief, research proposal, data collection, data analysis and evaluation and, finally, preparation and presentation of research report.

Problem definition may encompass a need for information on the performance of services, behaviour of users or clients, or the attitudes, perceptions and motivations of those users. The problem may centre on the behaviour and performance of competitors, or there may be a requirement to identify gaps in services or to seek potential solutions in a problematical situation. Objectives must be clear: the rationale for doing the research must be plain to all involved and this transparency will be invaluable in using the research findings effectively at a later stage.

The value of the required information needs to be assessed against the cost of collecting it, and the assessment of risk involved in not obtaining data must be addressed. Opportunity loss, i.e. the risk of loss involved in taking one decision rather than another, can be calculated statistically. Given a decent base of information, decisions will be taken very much more rationally. Research objectives will shape not only what information is collected, but the way in which the information is collected, in order that the level of required accuracy is achieved. The method of analysing results should lead easily to the effective presentation of the findings.

There is an enormous amount of information readily available from sources already in existence, available ever more readily via the internet: internal library or information service records; government publications, particularly statistical surveys from central offices of statistics; commercial market reports and analyses from companies such as Mintel or the Economist Intelligence Unit; trade and professional association yearbooks and directories. The major research agencies with websites, in addition to Mintel and ECI, with which the librarian and information professional should become familiar are Euromonitor, MORI, AC Nielsen, NOP and Verdict. The identification and collection of secondary data from such sources should prove no problem for the information professional.

Commissioning market research

Primary data collection should be left to the market research professionals. *Marketing research for managers* (Crouch and Housden, 1996) offers a detailed and accessible guide to the whole field of commissioning marketing research for those with little knowledge and less confidence. Commissioning a 'made to measure' survey is likened to the decision to buy a new suit, for example, and the overall aim is 'to enable the non-research manager to become a more informed research user and buyer, and to equip him or her with appropriate criteria for judging research quality' (Crouch and Housden, 1996, 77).

The Market Research Society is the incorporated professional body in the UK for those using market research techniques for marketing, social and economic research. The main aim of the Society, supported by a well-documented code of conduct, is 'to ensure the maintenance of professional standards in the practice of market research of all kinds'.

To ensure value from a market research supplier, librarians and information professionals must be equal partners in a dialogue with the researchers and see themselves as professional clients. The relevant types of research will be discussed between the librarians or information professionals and the market researchers, although the design of the research instruments would be best left to the market research professionals. The research supplier must be involved from the earliest stages of planning. They will help develop the research programme, but can only do that if they fully understand the context within which they are working. This applies not only to information service work: libraries have changed immensely in recent years and where traditional images of a library service are held by a researcher there is a danger that this could interfere with their creative thinking. Research suppliers will also be able to advise on cost-effective methods of obtaining the required information if they are aware of budget constraints from the beginning. It is essential to allow sufficient time for planning, if changes and expense are to be kept to a minimum. The nature of the report required should be made clear too; the following notes on methods will aid the librarian and information professional in digesting such reports as well as planning the research, but it is advisable to ask for an avoidance of jargon.

It may be possible to collect all kinds of information that it would be nice to know, but that become expendable when a price tag is put on them. Beware too, how easily analysis paralysis may set in. 'Findings are being analysed' can become a subconscious excuse for delaying decisions.

Building a relationship with research suppliers involves giving the suppliers feedback on their reports, and letting them know what happens. It makes sense to stay with a research supplier who has done a good job, because they are then better equipped to know the library and information world; there is less learning time involved in each project and the library or information service achieves the role of important client.

Market research techniques

The traditional scientific method of experimentation involves investigating matched groups – one a control group, others subjected to variables – that can then be measured to evaluate whether the effects of the variables can be said to be significantly different. Researching a market can take a number of forms: experimentation, observation and surveys are commonly found.

Experimentation

Methods of collecting data for library and information services will rarely need to include experimentation of the type where testers selected from the public will drink liquid, wash their hands, taste food or react to advertisements according to the new or improved product being tested. However, this method could be used where, perhaps, a university library planning to reorganize circulation, shelving and seating areas might complete one floor only in the new arrangement and test users' reactions before proceeding further.

Observation

Observations, whether collected by people or mechanical and electronic methods, measure overt behaviour only, e.g. an electronic eye may count traffic entry or exit points, or a researcher may observe how users respond physically to particular stimuli: a barrier, a notice, temperatures, etc. Supermarkets use cameras to observe customer eye movements and place goods accordingly and even eye-pupil size can be measured since this indicates rate of interest. The rousing music that accompanies the supermarket shopper at peak periods is replaced by more soothing, leisurely tunes come the quiet days of the week, encouraging the shopper to linger and presumably buy more. All this is based on observing how people respond to different stimuli.

Surveys

Surveys, beloved of the library profession, are widely used in many research situations but often badly executed. Surveys are really descriptive research and should be used to find out about users' knowledge, beliefs, behaviour, preferences or satisfaction rates. Personal interview, mail, telephone or the internet can be used to conduct surveys. Pilot surveys will play a helpful part in the successful operation of a major survey and careful design of the sampling procedures is essential. The sample frame, i.e. the list from which potential respondents will be drawn – it could be an electoral roll or membership list – needs to be up to date and accurate. To obtain a representative sample, opt for a simple, random probability method, which allows for the statistical calculation of sampling error so that every individual member of the population (or list) has an equal chance of selection.

A stratified random sample is just what it says: the population is divided into groups or strata, characterized by a common attribute, for example, age, income distribution or year of study, before the random sample is drawn.

Quota samples rely on convenience of access to the population and are not probability samples. They depend on the judgement of the interviewer. The street interview is of this type, where an interviewer will stop and question willing passers-by who fall into their required categories of so many of a particular age, sex or other category. And while the market research interviewer on the street is usually a woman, one suspects that this is more to do with the convenience of fitting domestic arrangements to the hours of work, rather than the enhanced communication skills of the female.

Questionnaires

Questionnaire design is a skill too little respected. Everybody from school-children to government departments appears to construct questionnaires confidently, a confidence very much misplaced in most cases. A carefully constructed questionnaire will elicit information to assist the decision-making process; a poorly designed questionnaire will often not collect the required data or will collect data in such a way as to lead to misleading conclusions.

To avoid pitfalls, a pilot questionnaire will help, for example, by highlighting areas of ambiguity in questions that need to be uniformly understood. Questionnaires can be of the self-completion type or used in the interview situation. Where the interviewer function is to read questions to, and record answers from, respondents, potentially inaccurate inferences will be reduced. An indication of the time needed to complete a questionnaire will encourage respondents, as will some form of incentive. General questions will ease the respondent into the survey, while classification questions, e.g. age, sex, socioeconomic questions, should be left to the end as they can be perceived as intrusive by some respondents.

The form the response to a question takes should allow for ease of collation and analysis. Open-ended questions, such as 'What do you think about the information service?', will be difficult for the respondent to answer, since much more information is needed, due to the question's imprecise nature. A dichotomous question that only allows for a yes or no answer will collect data easily. A multiple-choice question will allow for much more flexibility, thus, 'What age group are you in?' allows for several bands of answer. (The classic nightmare is to allow response bands to overlap, e.g. under 20 can be followed by 20–25, but 16–20 should not be followed by 20–25.) Questions that call for perception answers are rarely successful, e.g. 'How far do you live from the branch library?' is difficult for most people to answer, whereas many will remember their post or zip code, a much more accurate measure for data collection. The need to omit jargon or technical terms if respondents are not likely to have specific knowledge is obvious, but too often questions will include an unnoticed negative, e.g. 'Would you prefer not to have library fines?', or ask two questions in one, e.g. 'Would you like the information unit to open on Tuesday or Wednesday evening?' Sequential bias should also be avoided; initial questions can change a respondent's perception and alter responses to later questions. Vocabulary used can alter responses too, a question using 'should not be allowed' will be answered differently from one using 'should be prohibited'. In all cases it should be made clear who is operating the questionnaire and that personal information, if given, will be confidential.

Data should be collected, where possible, in a machine-readable form to enable faster collation of results, enabling valuable time to be concentrated on the analysis of results instead.

Focus groups

Focus group discussions, where a small group of people are brought together to discuss a concept, brand or product, traditionally were conducted at the same time as quantitative research, but the trend is now quite clearly for organizations to conduct these discussion groups after the tabulation of research results in order to provide insight into why the results were achieved. Lambin (2000, 148) also supports the view that 'the group interview is a superb mechanism for generating hypotheses when little is known about the problem under study'. Focus group discussions are commonly videoed as well as audio-recorded today.

SERVQUAL

The marketing research oriented SERVQUAL technique is aimed at identifying the gaps between customer expectations of service and their perceptions of actual service delivery. Customers complete a set of statements related to tangibles such as appearance, reliability (accuracy and dependability), responsiveness (promptness and helpfulness), assurance (credibility, competence and security) and empathy (communications and customer understanding). Rates of customer satisfaction are one outcome of SERVQUAL testing. More importantly it can identify areas where managers have misunderstood the market and are delivering what they think the customers want, when their customers actually want something quite different. Service quality specifications may not be carrying through into the delivery of services or the organization's communications may be giving a skewed picture of what the customer can realistically expect.

Mystery shoppers

Mystery shoppers can perform a useful function in the research process. A reader or user who is pretending to be genuine can test the reality of service provision and report back to management. These are snapshots of service provision, if done over time, at different venues and performed by 'mystery shoppers' in various guises, which can add to a rich picture of service delivery.

Other techniques

Other techniques for collecting opinions and attitude responses call for specialist operation and implementation. *Word association* calls for an analysis of the actual words respondents react to, and also the time gap before the response. *Sentence-completion methods* need to record all initial responses. *Story completion* asks respondents to complete the incomplete story presented to them, while *picture completion* asks respondents to fill in an empty speech balloon in a picture where two characters are presented, one having a speech balloon already filled in. *Thematic apperception* tests ask respondents to make up a story about a picture presented to them.

Obviously, all of these take skill in collection and analysis of responses. It is much easier to use questionnaires with closed-end questions, using such devices as a Likert scale, which gives a statement to which the respondent indicates the amount of agreement or disagreement on a semantic differential scale.

Nevertheless, the use of more unusual methods is worth considering. One of the UK national clearing banks was horrified to discover what non-users really thought about banks, by using the 'draw a person' (DAP) technique. Respondents were asked to draw a bank-teller. Not only were the graphic representations unsmiling, frowning, downright off-putting individuals, many respondents also drew strong black lines in front of the faces: a clear indication, unpalatable though it may have been, of how banks and their staff were perceived by the public. Hence we now have new bank images of open counters, named staff, customer-care programmes and user-friendly atmospheres. Libraries and information services might be surprised by the results of a similar exercise and pleasantly surprised; the so-called traditional librarian image myth is very largely perpetuated by the profession itself.

Web market research

The effectiveness of web marketing can be researched both offline by conventional methods and online, either by the automatic collection via software of web metrics (measurements by another name) or by using e-mail. Chaffey et al. (2000, Chapter 12) provide an excellent, non-technical framework to the various approaches. They concentrate on:

- *Capture* – how effective are the offline and online promotion methods used in attracting users to a site?
- *Content* – how well are users supported in ease of use as well as information?
- *Customer orientation* – is the site suited to the target audience: is it relevant, up to date and accurate?
- *Community and interactivity* – how are the individual user's needs provided for in community and interactive facilities on the site?

Online questionnaires and online focus groups are commonplace today, but it is worth remembering that the nature of the internet protects the individual user identity, unless the user has registered for use on the site, i.e. given permission (Godin, 1999). The use of registration with a password and of cookies, the small text files that are stored on a user's computer so that further visits to a particular site begin to build up a profile of the user, can enable the collection of web metrics to what is becoming a worrying degree when implications for privacy are considered.

It is worth bearing in mind, too, that 'when developing metric programmes the objective should be to assess the contribution of the web site to the business rather than to evaluate the web site in isolation' (Chaffey et al., 1999, 397).

Librarians and information professionals need market research to reach and serve their markets effectively. Valuable resources are squandered where sound data and information are not the bedrock of decision making. It is false economy to under-resource market research or to attempt in-house sourced activity where the expertise and time is not adequate. Co-operation with other organizations, authorities, departments and professional colleagues will often provide mutually beneficial opportunities for useful research activities. As markets become more competitive, libraries and information centres must meet market needs in a much more personal and precise way and deploy their

resources effectively as they do so. Market research will help them to identify their markets' characteristics and needs, and marketing research will help
them to identify the effectiveness of their marketing decision-making.

References and further reading

Asta, G. and Federighi, P. (eds) (2000) *The public and the library: reading, information and job guidance* (The European Commission Socrates Adult
Education Project), Edizione Polistampa.

Brassington, F. and Pettit, S. (2000) *Principles of marketing*, 2nd edn, Pitman.

Carson, D. et al. (2001) *Qualitative marketing research*, Sage Publications.

Chaffey, D. et al. (2000) *Internet marketing: strategy, implementation and practice*,
Financial Times/Prentice Hall.

Chisnall, P. M. (1997) *Marketing research*, McGraw-Hill; 6th edn, 2001.

Crouch, S. and Housden, M. (1996) *Marketing research for managers*, 2nd edn,
Butterworth-Heinemann on behalf of The Chartered Institute of Marketing; 3rd edn, 1999.

Fuld, L. M. (1992) Achieving total quality through intelligence, *Long Range
Planning*, **25** (1), 109–15.

Godin, S. (1999) *Permission marketing*, Simon and Schuster.

Kotler, P. (2000) *Marketing management: the millennium edition*, 10th edn, Prentice Hall.

Lambin, J.-J. (2000) *Market-driven management*, Macmillan Press.

O'Connor, J. and Galvin, E. (2001) *Marketing in the digital age*, 2nd edn, Pearson.

Orna, E. with Stevens, G. (1997) *Managing information for research*, Open
University Press.

Piercy, N. (1992) *Market-led strategic change*, Butterworth-Heinemann; 3rd edn,
2001.

Wright, L. T. and Crimp, M. (2000) *The market research process*, Prentice Hall.

9
CORPORATE IDENTITY AND CORPORATE IMAGE

Identity is what we are, image is what we appear to be.

Corporate identity policy aims at communicating an appropriate message about an organization, its intents and purposes, internally and externally, to all who come into contact with the organization. Corporate identity philosophy puts the user at the centre of strategy.

The prime objective of corporate image is to *visibly* design, package and deliver quality services to the user, client or customer. Its main aim is the shaping of customer perception.

The objectives of this chapter are:

- to examine the relevance of corporate identity and corporate image to libraries and information centres
- to question whether librarians and information professionals are in an identity crisis
- to explore the role of names, symbols, logos and design in promoting corporate image
- to introduce the ACID test concept of corporate identity:
  - **A**ctual identity (what the library or information service is)
  - **C**ommunicated identity (communication controlled by the library or information service and non-controllable communication)
  - **I**deal identity (the very best image possible for the library or information service)
  - **D**esired identity (management's vision, may well be pure fantasy).

The importance of corporate identity and corporate image

Perhaps 'there is no more dramatic and truly horrific example of corporate identity at its most glittering, powerful and hypnotic than that of the Third Reich . . . colours, symbols, buildings, uniforms and signs (Olins, 1978, 22). The Church also, through the centuries, has evolved a system of rituals, buildings, symbols and uniforms, as have the armed forces.

These examples serve to emphasize the sheer power of corporate identity since their mere mention almost certainly arouses strong images and responses.

Companies and organizations work hard to engender a strong corporate image: Kodak, Marks and Spencer and ICI will all provoke a similar response in whichever country they are mentioned, so strong is the image of the company. They sometimes make expensive mistakes in the process. Newspapers reported gleefully that British Airways spent several millions of pounds on shortening the skirts of stewardesses to show how modern the company is, that tail planes were being repainted at enormous cost because the carrier could not be identified from the modern art depicted. ICI changed a straight line to a wavy one on the logo and also attracted adverse media comment. This window dressing may appear to be trivial, but it is a reflection of how an organization will consistently and continually endeavour to nourish and burnish public perceptions of its worth. If the mission, however, is no more than pretty words on a shopfront or website, then no matter how large or well established the organization may be, that organization will deteriorate and crumble. Logos and symbols are part of the global system of communication but they must communicate genuine quality and commitment.

Is it not time for libraries and information centres, too, to pay more attention to such issues?

Core values

Robert Woodruff, former Coca-Cola president, is famous for saying 'Coca-Cola is a religion' (Schmidt, 1995, 3). He was right to identify the cultural impact of his brand, possibly the greatest in Western post-war culture according to Schmidt. But what is vital to acknowledge also is the hard-hitting reality that the cultural identity of the organization itself impacts on its corporate image. The library or information service that is not clear about its objectives, that communicates badly with its own staff, will not find it easy to communicate a strong image to the outside world. This is no place for the old complaint 'This would be a great place to work if it weren't for the readers.' As Johnson (1999, 138) says: 'You do not have to do this – survival is not compulsory.'

It is impossible to hide behind public relations and design programmes, however good they may be of themselves. When core values are wrong, then the public sooner or later will become aware of this and in the internet age, as some of our largest corporations have found to their cost, information travels fast as well as far and an image is easily tarnished. Crucial to the success of a corporate identity policy is to acknowledge: 'If it touches the customer, it's a marketing issue. And, of course, if it's a marketing issue, it's part of the corporate image management process' (Howard, 1998, 113).

Wally Olins (1989, 7), deemed to be a doyen of the corporate identity business, says that 'purpose and belonging are the two facets of identity. Every organization is unique, and the identity must spring from the organization's own roots, its personality, its strengths and weaknesses.'

Research by Ind (1990, 77) concluded that 'what really determines the strength of the organizational identity is the extent to which values are commonly held in an organization . . . [that] the values are clearly defined and supported and endorsed not only by words, but also, more importantly, by actions and leadership'.

Corporate identity

But why might librarians and information professionals concern themselves with corporate identity? Corporate behaviour is going to evolve as a result of group behaviour. The issue is whether to control and develop group behaviour and visual trappings to affect relationships with users and other groups to the benefit of the library and information service.

A corporate identity programme will increase the visibility of the library or information service, enhance perceived value and promote services with greater impact. Corporate identity aims at communicating an appropriate message about the library or information service, its intents and purpose, to its many publics, internal and external. The message has to be clear, cohesive and consistent if it is to influence those publics' perceptions of the library and information service. When that message is via the internet, users, readers and clients need to meet a consistent message, typeface, logo and content, so that a solid, familiar feeling is created (Janal, 2000, 9).

> The fundamental idea behind an identity programme is that in everything the organization does, everything it owns, and everything it produces it should project a clear idea of what it is and what its aims are. The most significant way in which this can be done is by making everything in and around the organization – its products, buildings, communications and behaviour – consistent in purpose and performance. (Olins, 1999, 10)

The library or information service that is part of a large organization with a good corporate identity strategy, implemented effectively, may very well find that it is hidden as a result. A check of signs, reception areas, staff clothing, badges, business cards, stationery, letterheads, memos, compliments slips, envelopes, forms, publications and web pages within a website will quickly show whether the library and information service has a visible presence or whether it is only the parent organization that is highlighted. Customizing to promote the library identity, to enhance the image of the information service, should be done in conjunction with the organization's marketing or communications department. For three reasons: the resulting image will be professional, the costs are likely to be borne by the parent organization, and it's an effective promotional public relations ploy within the organization.

Identity crisis?

Librarians and information professionals do have an identity crisis. Where does their identity lie? The image of the library has been forged over centuries, from the Library of Thebes with its legend over the portal, 'The healing place of the soul', to the information-technology palaces of today. The public perception of the library profession is largely honed by the media's presentation of public libraries. 'Goldilocks was a juvenile delinquent' heralded a workshop on censorship organized by the American Library Association Intellectual Freedom Committee. Should we be surprised that the media perpetuates an image of the public library as censorious with headlines of similar ilk? Why do we rarely read, for example, of the many successful drop-in schemes for young people run by public libraries? Is it surprising that the image is confused?

What do professionals believe is the corporate identity of their membership body? What identity would an individual library or information service wish to promote? Does the parent organization or authority have a corporate identity policy to which it must comply? When school libraries today are so obviously learning organizations, why are they still treated as the Cinderella department when school budgets are allocated? Academic libraries are increasingly the heart of an electronic campus, so why does 'university library' still conjure up thoughts of learned, musty tomes? In a dynamic era when information is a valued commercial resource, why do business information units have to struggle to make the case for more resources?

Is it inevitable that libraries and information services should have such a poor image? Or do they have a poor image at all? Truth to tell, setting aside the above, there is not much real evidence that libraries are poorly perceived. Much of the commentary comes, in fact, from the library profession itself, which has appeared determined for too long to perpetuate the doubtful myth of the timid and fusty librarian. Accountants, bankers and lawyers have all been portrayed in literature, film or television as badly, or as well, as librarians. Do they feel the need to polish the public perception of their professions? The workloads of the ombudsmen who now exist as arbitrators or watchdogs of these professions suggest that they should. But has this engendered a crisis of confidence in their ranks? No, they are moving on. A growing number of professional firms, and some banks, now employ image consultants in order to create an effective individual identity that will differentiate them from the somewhat boring, or even tarnished, image projected by their profession.

The mission of libraries and information services must be to build and sustain a reputation for quality and user and client commitment. 'i' for information has become an international icon; it needs to be joined by other equally recognized and respected library symbols.

It is important to remember that images persist because people are selective in their reception of information, filtering it in the light of 'what they already know'. Changing an image, therefore, is a slow process.

Corporate identity strategy

Corporate identity strategy is the establishment of an organization's personality by means of external signs and behaviour such as the use of logos, the appearance of premises, inside and outside, publications and publicity in corporate style, vehicle liveries and so on. But it is not a mere cosmetic exercise, even though it involves enhancing image through tangible objects. Corporate identity is an important element in the culture of an organization; it is all-pervasive and it needs to derive from mission, objectives and strategy. Bernstein (1991, 241) said that corporate identity implementation cannot happen unless the organization 'improves its strategic thinking, organization structure and internal communications. A professional corporate identity programme is thus both the result of change and the catalyst of change.'

Corporate identity strategy must also be co-ordinated and consistent. An organization:

can only adjust its identity properly to express its personality; or, if necessary, re-examine its personality. To attempt an 'image change' by means of a new logo, slogan and colour scheme unrelated to the character of the company can bring at best only short-term success. Painting the privy won't cure the plumbing.

(Bernstein, 1991, 241)

It would be interesting to have Bernstein's views on the companies using feng shui consultants to harmonize their environments and encourage positive energies. In Singapore, the Suntec City commercial complex is built as a giant hand, the palm of the hand holding the Fountain of Prosperity. United Overseas Bank (UOB), in the same city, delayed the inauguration of its new skyscraper office blocks two years in order to coincide with the arrival of the Year of the Dragon, 2000, which was expected to lead to opportunities in business and to spectacular achievement and success. These companies are presenting strong cultural messages about their identity to their markets.

At the heart of corporate identity strategy the library and information service needs coherence, symbolism and positioning (Olins, 1989, 148). First, the organization wants to present itself as clear and comprehensible, Second, the organization wants to symbolize its ethos, its attitudes, so that everyone who works for it can share the same spirit and then communicate it to all the people who deal with the organization. Third, the organization wants to differentiate itself and its products from those of its competitors in the marketplaces.

Customer education must be also be a prime objective, argue Zeithaml and Bitner (2000, 407); services marketing communications must be integrated and managed as they are crucial to corporate identity programme management. If customers, or users, are unclear about how a service will be provided or perhaps are inexperienced in using a service, for example burgeoning online internet services or intranet facilities, then their perceptions of the service and its overall image will be very much affected. Where such users are well informed, are given clear guidelines or instructions, are encouraged to approach staff for further information or training or support, the image will be very much more positive.

Culture change

There is risk involved in organizational identity or cultural change within organizations: staff may see change as artificial, especially if corporate design programmes appear completely 'unrelated to the actual shambles they work in' (Bernstein, 1991, 161).

An empirical study to demonstrate how cultural change might be managed in response to new marketing strategies and identity values, conducted by Mühlbacher et al. (1987), discovered major differences between senior executives' and employees' motives. Senior executives had a high level of identification with top management goals: they sought to innovate and promote teamwork, but an information system came fairly low in their priorities. By comparison, employees saw the good flow of information as vital and it came high on their lists after a pleasant working environment. Jose Chacel Tuya, Director of Communications at Iberdrola, presented a similar picture of his findings in 2001 and listed 20 accusations made by employees against management, including deliberate obscurity of communications, talking to the media before staff, evasiveness and the encouragement of second-hand information.

Working towards a situation where there is a congruency of views takes time, but there is little point in attempting to implement a corporate identity programme without regard to the culture of the organization. Bernstein (1991, 53) warned: 'Knowing oneself is hard enough. Articulating that knowledge is tougher. And being able to relate one's beliefs and aspirations to society, particularly a society in ferment, makes the task quite daunting.'

In a public debate pursued on the internet and in the printed media, *The profits and principles debate*, Shell (2001) is seeking to confirm its corporate identity as a company concerned with society and human rights as well as profits. Interestingly, Shell stresses its commitment to its employees first: 'At Shell, we are committed to support fundamental human rights and have made this commitment in our published Statement of General Business Principles. It begins with our own people, respecting their rights as employees.' Where are the debates, the public statements from our libraries, our librarians, our professional associations of information professionals? Where are the attempts to seek sponsorship or government funding to make public their ethos, their aims? This is not to say that they do not exist, it is a plea to make them more public, to engender a corporate identity, to fashion a profession proud of its calling.

Costs

The value of an overall policy becomes apparent when one considers how many different forces are at work in the design elements of most libraries and information services. These range through architects and builders, to interior designers, purchase departments, printers of everything from stationery to promotional posters, signmakers and workwear manufacturers. The cheering factor is that all of these elements are costs that will be met anyway; thus the implementation costs of a corporate identity policy will be very little more in the long term. Dramatic and immediate changes in style will obviously be costly, but in most libraries and information services it is much more likely to be a case of appraisal, reorganization and positive projections of existing practices. And a cheering example, when FedEx was rebranded, their aeroplanes were painted white instead of dark blue as part of the corporate identity campaign; dark colours absorb heat, so as a result of the new white livery there were enormous savings on air conditioning. The savings were so large they paid for the corporate identity consultants' fees for the first year (Middleton, 2001, 40). Something as simple as standardizing on stationery will cut costs as a result of bulk ordering, corporate livery colours throughout the library system will do the same. Colour psychology will dictate the rate of effective responses to a website, and money spent on design could make the difference to the survival of an information service.

What's in a name?

The best names communicate the idea of the core benefits offered by the services; thus the inclusion of the words 'library' or 'information' is important but is not paramount. Consider how some commercial names attempt to communicate key benefits creatively: Autoglass, Weight Watchers, Toys 'R' Us, Interflora, Wash & Go. Consider too the following, which give no indication of the type of product or benefit: Black and Decker, Dulux, Heinz, Kodak, Playtex, Wedgwood. Yet the customer recognition rate for all of them is invariably high. The marketing budgets for these companies contain a high proportion of spending on promotion of the company name or identity. Companies may decide on corporate promotion and emphasize the company name accordingly on all of their products or they may decide to promote individual brands heavily, with little or no indication of the company name. In fact, there are a range of options on identity promotion in the marketplace. The librarian and information professional needs to make major decisions on identity and what needs to be promoted in whatever sector they find themselves operating. Marshall (2001, 119) discovered that many academic library directors 'were uncomfortable with the public relations aspects of their job', one commented that he believed 'that it is a tactic used by big companies or government to hide the truth'. He may be right on that score, but were he and his colleagues to put the user at the centre of their thinking then many of their misgivings would melt away.

The name of the parent organization or authority will need to be indicated, for internal and external publics alike. The University Library, the Public Library, the Information Unit, do not give many clues. Where a specific name is already used and is comparatively well known, it might be argued that place of origin is not so vital, but outside of the academic world, what proportion of the public recognizes the Bodleian Library? It is important that they do: a generous proportion of the income raised by this apparently traditional institution comes via non-traditional library products and services, as a glance at their catalogue of goods will testify.

Corporate identity policy will demand that the new name appears everywhere possible: fascias, mobile service vans, stationery, carrier bags, serviettes in the library café, etc., so time has to be taken over any change of name: it is a costly business. Consultation with staff and users must be part of the process. Many a reasonable-sounding name has had to be discarded because it results in an unfortunate acronym; discard the unwieldy and the overlong too. If users are not sure, they will invent names, not all calculated to enhance a good image, and non-users will remain just that.

Where the corporate identity policy of the parent body dictates the name to be used, there may be little choice over matters of design either; however, it is important to fight for an identity, whether through name or logo, for the library or information service. 'Libraries' are disappearing in the UK: in the public sphere, they are part of an amorphous mass of leisure, recreation and arts; in the universities, information services is an umbrella term for central services, and in other spheres, information professionals are not, on the whole, likely to be working in 'libraries'.

Design

The library and information service will be aiming at projecting a reputation for quality, and image is a vital component of quality in the eyes of today's markets. Visual presentation is crucial, since it is well established that over 80% of what is learned comes to us through sight. It follows that design, colour and typefaces must be considered with care for all aspects of visual presentation, including the external and internal environment, publications, communications of all kinds and all distribution services.

The employment of a professional designer will be money well spent. 'Most people coming for the first time to an activity where decisions on colour, shape and style are called for are reluctant to trust their own judgement. It's bad enough picking a tie,' said Olins in 1978 (189). His conclusion still holds good today when not only are do-it-yourself stores flourishing, but so are a myriad of television programmes and magazines on style and use of colour.

Librarians are accused of hiding behind subdued good taste, which is not necessarily such a bad thing to be accused of. There is a growing disquiet about visual pollution and design consultants as well as city planners are attempting to counteract the despoliation of the environment. A measure of that concern is the control of the outdoor advertising industry in the USA by the Highway Beautification Act. Yet all libraries and information services want to be considered efficient, forward-looking and progressive, with an excellent customer-care interface. How is the library or information service going to stand out? Good professional design will provide the answer. The value of the designer's work must be exploited to the full; consistency in visual communications is vital. A manual of how the chosen designs and colours should be incorporated in all types of product, communication or activity is an invaluable tool and should be part of the contract. Such a manual will support the library's aim for quality and consistency in style, and provide a hallmark for the information unit's work.

Typefaces

This is probably one area where librarians could have more knowledge than designers in terms of the choice available, but it is the designer who is creating the total image and will be looking for specific qualities in the typeface to enhance the overall design.

The style of typeface conveys as much as the words used about the services on offer. Contrast a clean, clear Helvetica with say a heavy Gothic: each in the appropriate setting will convey its subliminal message: 'We are modern, forward looking' or 'We believe in traditional values'. The use of capital letters or lower case also makes a difference. One word in capitals looks powerful and is easily understood: 'STOP' works on an international scale; 'Stop' is nowhere near as effective. Conversely, putting all the message into capitals makes the content much more difficult to decipher. Consider 'NO BOOKS MAY BE RETURNED OR ISSUED IN THE TEN MINUTES BEFORE THE LIBRARY IS DUE TO CLOSE'; apart from the command tone of the words, the message is difficult to digest. Script presents even more problems, not just of legibility and image; handwriting analysis is now used everywhere and even the general public can translate the various clues.

The colours used and the weight chosen will also affect design and message dramatically. The corporate identity manual will detail what is acceptable use: a simple 'Let's have the logo in red, for a change' could be a costly mistake if the manual stipulates black or green only, because red is not going to work in some way or the image will be distorted by its use. Be warned though that it is impossible to cover all the bright ideas that staff might dream up at a later date. A web page designer is also needed, to cope with the availability of colours via various technical systems – an unbecoming sludge does nothing to promote identity if a particular system cannot cope with the glorious multicoloured original.

It does not need a designer to decide that all signs in the library or information unit should use the same typeface. A speedy and cost-effective way of tidying up the working environment, it looks efficient and is much more helpful to the user.

Logos

Logo is short for logotype. According to dictionary definitions, it is a single piece of type bearing a non-heraldic device, chosen as the badge of an organization and used in advertisements and on notepaper, etc. A logo is so much more emotive than that straightforward explanation; it embodies all that the organization wants to say about itself. It is an emblem to convey instantly the purpose and personality of the library or information service.

A logo should symbolize the organization it represents in such a way that an immediate link can be made. Selame and Selame (1988, 110) say that it is 'an immutable law: any symbol or trademark that requires more than a few seconds of thought to get its message across is not doing what it is supposed to do. What characterises a successful corporate symbol or trademark is its innate simplicity, its ability to communicate quickly.' Probably one of the best-known symbols worldwide has been Mr Bibendum, the Michelin Man, who provokes a smile as well as getting his message across. Symbols are tremendously powerful; consider the Red Cross, an organization that uses one of the most powerful symbols of all time. Clear, unambiguous, original and distinctive, the symbol has meaning and purpose for the people within the organization and outside

A logo carries a responsibility to be functional. It should be adaptable to enable it to serve as a unifier in all the elements of a corporate identity programme, from huge fascia to personal badges.

A logo that is easy to recognize and pleasing to the eye, utilizing simple graphics, also needs to reproduce well. It needs to stand out in competing surroundings in whatever material it appears on, whether glass, wood, metal, stone or paper, and whether it is embossed, embedded or raised. A slogan can form part of a logo, but slogans are better avoided in the main. 'Information for the millennium' sounds dated already. 'We're getting there' will have a decidedly hollow ring in a few years' time.

Logos can appear in a whole variety of effective graphic forms. Words within a seal shape, such as used by Ford, are popular, and embellished with gold or silver further a classic image. Monograms, for example as used by IBM, are seen everywhere, but there needs to be heavy promotional spending to ensure that the users know who is behind the initials. A glyph or pictograph – the Shell shell or the British Woolmark ball of yarn are examples – has better recognition qualities than a purely abstract form, which needs to be established through extensive promotion. It is also unlikely that a logo that needs expansive explanation, especially of the 'forward leaning is to suggest the vigour and progress of the organization' ilk, will have any chance of success in the marketplace and the minds of users.

Although often spoken of as if the same thing trademarks are different from logos. A trademark is legally registered today, although originally they were established by use. It can be a word, name, picture, symbol, device, or any combination of these, used by merchants or manufacturers to identify their goods and distinguish them from those made by competitors. Trademarks have been discovered dating back as far as 4000 BC: the signed ceramics found in Yang-Shaots'un (Hunan) are the first recorded goods to carry a trademark. The Phoenicians and Romans used them, medieval artisans, and later the powerful guilds, used them to protect the reputation of their goods.

Will today's logos and trademarks have the same powerful impact? It would be difficult to find a symbol that epitomizes 'library' from past eras; alas, it's not much easier to come up with examples today.

Uniforms or workwear

The majority of service organizations now dress their employees as part of the corporate look. It might be argued that libraries, as did banks, had a sort of uniform in the dress code that prevailed for centuries. However, the dark, sensible colours of the bank tellers (selected not to show ink stains and reduce wash frequency) have disappeared in a flurry of much brighter plumage. This clothing is not labelled a uniform: it is called workwear, as in leisurewear or evening wear. Does this make the concept any more palatable to staff in the library or information service? It would seem not in the case of libraries, where even name badges have caused opposition and controversy.

The main purpose of a uniform is to identify staff, although hospitals are among the institutions to use uniforms to indicate status also. It is especially useful to be able to identify people who are members of staff in an environment where staff are not fixed behind a desk – curiously as they generally are in a bank or building society. This is further proof of how important to the corporate image the uniform is held to be.

Corporate clothing today is well designed, made of good-quality materials, suits the working environment and projects a modern, professional approach. It can communicate the corporate identity clearly and, at its best, promotes the image of a team. However, it can have the effect of suppressing individuality. Uniform clothing may promote uniform behaviour; an individual's personal behaviour and appearance is to a large extent subdued when in uniform.

Perhaps here we have the reason for the apparent antagonism to the idea of uniforms in library situations. The evidence from Japanese management, who dress in identical fashion to the workforce, is that this promotes harmony and a true corporate identity. If in truth libraries are centres for freedom of thought, where does that leave uniform dressing and, more importantly, corporate image? Corporate identity is what the library is, what it stands for; uniform dressing could provoke the wrong image.

It would seem a sensible compromise to ask staff to wear badges with at least the name of the service shown so that users can approach them with confidence. Equally, if the librarian–user relationship is seen to be a professional one, there is a case for names to be used too. The information service will probably have fewer staff, who are well known to users. They may have to wear security identity badges at all times. It will reflect the style of the service if first names are included, even if this is not the company norm.

If you do decide to enter the minefield of corporate clothing, prior consultation with staff is imperative. It is a costly decision – how many uniforms per person, how many changes per season, etc. and, above all, people do come in a variety of shapes and sizes, which are not constant either. In addition, it is worth remembering that sexual discrimination is also a factor, employees will need to be treated in comparable fashion regardless of their gender.

Lessons from the marketplace

Governments are among those operating corporate identity programmes. Canada provides an excellent example of how communication processes have been simplified within government departments and a nationwide identity programme implemented. The Canadian Ministry of Health and Human Services became Health Canada, the Canadian Ministry of Air Transport became Air Canada and a single maple leaf appeared everywhere as the instantly recognizable symbol for the country.

A smallish cog in a mighty big wheel, Waterstone's in the UK retained its very clear identity as the bookseller 'with bibliophile sensibility' within W. H. Smith. Alan Giles, Managing Director of Waterstone's in the early 1990s, emphasized the paramount importance of customer service saying: 'the way you make the brand come alive in-store is inextricably linked to the management culture of the shopfloor . . . staff are seen as the front line of Waterstone's marketing' (Benady, 1993, 20). Waterstone's successful marketing activities continue with their popular programmes of events, readings, author signings, review publications and catalogues. Librarians could borrow the philosophy: as Giles maintained (ibid.): 'books and authors are always newsworthy, so we benefit from a lot of PR coverage. And like other high street retailers, we can rely on our shop-fronts to act as poster sites.'

The ACID test

Librarians and information professionals might find it useful to consider the ACID test of corporate identity management from the International Centre for Corporate Identity Studies (Balmer and Soenen, 1999) before deciding on strategic change. The test explores Soul (core values and cultures), Mind (vision, philosophy, strategy) and Voice (all communications, direct and indirect). ACID investigates:

- **A**ctual identity – what the library or information service is, what the values of managers and staff are
- **C**ommunicated identity – includes both communication controlled by the library or information service and non-controllable communication such as media commentary, as well as existing reputation
- **I**deal identity – this would be the very best image possible of the library or information service in the eyes of its users and others in its sphere
- **D**esired identity – senior management's vision, may well be pure fantasy.

Finally, to succeed, a corporate identity programme must be truly integrated, it must involve every employee and every element of the library and information service, and it has to be communicated with consistency and commitment.

References and further reading

Balmer, J. M. T. (1998) Corporate identity and the advent of corporate marketing, *Journal of Marketing Management*, **14** (8), 963–96.

Balmer, J. M. T. and Soenen, G. B. (1999) The ACID test of corporate identity management, *Journal of Marketing Management*, **15** (1–3), 69–92.

Benady, A. (1993) How Alan Giles learned to love his brand, *Marketing*, (8 July), 20–1.

Bernstein, D. (1991) *Company image and reality: a critique of corporate communications*, Cassell Educational.

Chacel Tuya, J. L. (2001) El comunicador empresarial, *Empresa*, **4**, (July–August), 22–3.

Cornelissen, J. and Harris, P. (2001) The corporate identity metaphor: perspectives, problems and prospects, *Journal of Marketing Management*, **17** (1–2), 49–71.

Howard, S. (1998) *Corporate image management: a marketing discipline for the 21st century*, Butterworth-Heinemann.

Ind, N. (1990) *The corporate image: strategies for effective identity programmes*, Kogan Page.

Janal, D. S. (2000) *Dan Janal's guide to marketing on the internet*, John Wiley.

Johnson, B. (1999) *Introducing management: a development guide for new managers*, Butterworth-Heinemann.

Marshall, N. J. (2001) Public relations in academic libraries: a descriptive analysis, *Journal of Academic Librarianship*, **27** (2), 116–21.

Middleton, T. (2001) The name game, *Marketing Means Business for the CEO*, (Spring), 40–5.

Mühlbacher, H. et al. (1987) Successful implementation of new market strategies – a corporate culture perspective, *Journal of Marketing Management*, **3** (2), 205–17.

Olins, W. (1978) *The corporate personality: an inquiry into the nature of corporate identity*, Design Council.

Olins, W. (1989) *Corporate identity: making business strategy visible through design*, Thames and Hudson.

Olins, W. (1999) *The new guide to identity*, The Design Council.

Rowden, M. (2000) *The art of identity: creating and managing a successful corporate identity*, John Wiley.

Schmidt, K. (1995) *The quest for identity: corporate identity, strategies, methods and examples*, Cassell.

Selame, E. and Selame, J. (eds) (1988) *The company image: building your identity and influence in the marketplace*, John Wiley.

Shell (2001) Shell International Ltd, *The profits and principles debate*, available at Shell Centre, London SE1 7NA or at **www.shell.com**

Willmott, M. (2001) *Citizen brands: putting society at the heart of your business*, John Wiley.

Zeithaml, V. A. and Bitner, M. J. (2000) *Services marketing: integrating customer focus across the firm*, McGraw-Hill.

10
THE MARKETING PLAN

The marketing plan is a crucial step in marketing success for the library and information service. It must derive from strategic decisions based on answers to these major questions:

- What business are we in?
- What business do we want to be in?
- What are our priorities?

The marketing plan is a strategic document that will identify market position, state objectives, and outline how they will be achieved, resources required and results expected.

The objectives of this chapter are:

- to emphasize the need for marketing to be integral to strategy, structure and management of libraries and information centres
- to discuss the nature of the marketing plan as a strategic document and a blueprint for implementation
- to examine the planning process
- to aid librarians and information professionals prepare a marketing plan for libraries and information centres.

The reduced need for physical assets and disappearance of limitations imposed by geographical constraints, coupled with a demand for and ability to present instantaneous information, in a world that is a patchwork of information rich and populations deprived of literacy, make the roles of librarians and information professionals more challenging than ever. The preceding chapters have detailed why and how marketing is integral to the well-being, survival, development and growth of libraries and information centres.

Marketing planning needs to begin at the highest strategic level; the librarian and information professional must feed into that level of planning and feel comfortable with the idea of marketing themselves and their recommendations. Effective marketing planning depends on the extensive, existing strengths of librarians and information professionals, on their knowledge of users, stocks, services and staff capabilities, enhanced by a knowledge of marketing strategies and an appreciation of resource potential. The following is a discussion of how colleagues and senior management might be apprised of, and persuaded to support, marketing objectives through the presentation of a good marketing plan.

Preparing the plan

The library or information service marketing plan could be part of a larger corporate or institution plan. Conversely, the marketing plan of a smaller information consultancy can be presented, in its entirety, as a business plan, to bank managers or potential partners.

McDonald and Payne's (1998) *Marketing planning for services* is a useful, practical manual. Full of templates for the various steps needed, it is based on McDonald's *Marketing plans: how to prepare them, how to use them* (1999), which is invaluable.

The marketing plan needs to be thoroughly clear in communicating its intentions and it should be produced in a format that will allow it to be used by a multiple audience, from boardroom to functional level, as it becomes a working tool from a policy document. For all organizations, from multinational information service to small school library, the production and implementation of a sound marketing plan will reap exhilarating results.

The marketing plan is a *policy document*, taking as its starting point the mission, aims and objectives of the organization or institution. It is also a *strategic planning document*, which needs to address priorities and consequent allocation of resources in the light of external and internal variables. It should be a *management blueprint* too, in that it is also a *document about implementation*, setting out targets, how to reach them, who is responsible, the timetable involved and the budget devolved. It may include alternative solutions or an array of potential methodologies with reasons for the decisions made. Evaluation and performance measures must be built in and reporting lines clearly identified.

Ownership

It is important that a sense of collective ownership of the plan permeates the entire library or information centre staff structure: responsibility and creativity can only be fostered in an environment of shareholding and consultation and staff communication perspectives must be built into the planning process and the plan itself. Staff training in marketing should be part of the human resource element of the plan and must include all levels of staff. Inculcating the marketing ethos throughout the structure of the library and information centre and services is vital. It can be done via workshops, customer care programmes, market research, staff publications, noticeboards, competitions, awards, meetings with readers, suppliers and external clients, both real and virtual, focus groups, suggestion systems, the potential is huge in cultural change. It all needs resources and the plan should spell this out.

Gaining acceptance

Gaining acceptance of a marketing plan's recommendations is a challenge: the competition for resources is keen whatever the situation. McDonald and Payne (1998, 44) say:

the three most critical problems facing service organisations in their marketing planning are (in order of importance):

- hard to get consensus (co-operation)
- company isn't market oriented
- plans not taken seriously enough.

Most librarians and information professionals will recognize the truth of this and would benefit from the vast array of leadership advice available in the marketplace to better enable them to persuade colleagues and senior management of the value of their recommendations on strategy formulation, implementation and evaluation.

Audience

The marketing plan will be primarily aimed at an executive body, which will need to approve not only the resource implications, but the priorities and approaches defined by the plan. It is important to remember that the timetable for producing a marketing plan needs to build in the executive decision-making process, as well as the consultation processes in the early stages of development.

The structure and content of the final document need to take into account the kind of decision-making structure of the organization too. It is likely that the first stage of the plan's passage will be at a level where the executives or management team will be closely involved with the library or information service and will have a knowledge and understanding of the system and its environment. This is not likely to be the case as the plan proceeds: even where an organization is not particularly hierarchical in structure, senior executives may have limited knowledge of the library or information centre. Even in those cases where librarians and information officers are reaching the highest office, and there is a discernible trend here, the plan must speak clearly for itself and not be dependent on interpretation or need background explanation and defence.

Timescales

Change is inevitable and any plan needs to be flexible enough to adapt to contingencies. The strategic marketing plan may cover a three- to five-year period, in line with the institution's planning timescale. It will, of necessity, either include or generate subsets or mini-marketing plans, which will focus on a particular segment or service. Janal's (2000) 'online marketing business plan', for example, although in specific detail for commercial concerns, identifies useful ideas that non-profit-making ventures could utilize: distributing time sensitive information, a frequently asked questions response system and online support systems that release staff for higher-level enquiries. Often these mini-marketing plans will be more valuable if approached as one-year operational plans. It is vital, however, to dissuade any of the senior management team who think that it is possible to tackle a mini-marketing plan before developing the strategic marketing plan. That way lies disaster, not only in non-effective use of resources, but in dissipation of energies and motivation too.

The planning process

The planning process itself is comparatively easy to describe:

- Analyse the marketplace.
- Analyse the organization.
- Set objectives.
- Decide on strategies.
- Formulate tactics.

Also, in the development processes, aim throughout to:

- be consistent
- systemize information collection
- be specific
- quantify objectives
- share the creative processes.

This hides a mountain of work, a need for good marketing information systems, co-operation between levels of management and an acceptance of marketing philosophy. The librarian must work towards that acceptance, although it is easier in other information sectors where, whether in the public or private sector, there is a ready recognition of marketing effectiveness. The librarian, therefore, will need to be even sharper than his or her professional colleagues in information centres when it comes to providing evidence and reasoned argument, if marketing planning is to be transformed into activity and activity into success.

A useful argument is that the marketing plan is based on sound information, which has become, through a process of analysis and evaluation, competitive intelligence. It is therefore, in itself, competitive intelligence, since it includes trends analysis, business and competitor evaluation and management forecasting.

Promotion opportunity

The marketing plan is another opportunity for promotion and enhancing public relations. Marketing planning itself is a stimulating process: it is a motivator and activator and participants will not be wary of so-called 'planning blight' if activities and deadlines identified are progressed and met. Consultation improves awareness and affects image: it demonstrates that the library or information service has a sound future, for which it is planning effectively, and that it cares about what its users, readers, clients and suppliers think. While focus groups provide data to act on, consultation task groups provide friends and consortia to support, aid and abet the marketing process. Draft marketing planning documents presented to key personnel for comment can provide not only valuable feedback but even more valuable allies. The school football captain can be as valuable to the school librarian in this context as can the head teacher. Feedback in the form of interim reports provides the same kinds of opportunities for involving people and gaining their support.

Presenting the plan

The marketing plan is a tool too and must not be blunted by extraneous material. Only data that are needed should be included, and they should be presented in a fashion suited to the specific audience, i.e. marketing tactics are as essential in the plan's presentation as in its content.

Librarians and information professionals will be adept at the distillation and presentation of information, but they will need to think carefully before deciding how, where and when the marketing plan will be put forward most effectively. Positioning on the right agenda at the right time is crucial. If the plan is to appear as part of a series of such documents presented to an appropriate board or committee, how does it stand out? What makes its proposals attractive? Having it brought in by dancing girls is not the answer. What will work are:

- presentation in web format for the intranet, as well as hard copy
- professional appearance, both of presenter and plan
- discreet lobbying of appropriate board or committee members
- ensuring you receive an invitation to attend the deliberations, to introduce the plan and to answer questions raised
- priming committee members beforehand with answers to questions they might never have asked but for the timely nudge, in order to achieve awareness of issues you would like raised
- the prompt supply of any information asked for or promised.

Contents

A sound marketing plan will contain the following elements:

- an executive summary
- a brief statement of mission
- an analysis of the macro-environment
- a marketing audit, a SWOT analysis
- portfolio analysis

- specific objectives
- market analysis – segmentation
- proposed marketing strategies
- market research strategies
- marketing mixes recommended
- evaluation methods
- timetable
- budget.

The executive summary

An overview of the plan, it should encapsulate the plan's objectives and content to enable a quick grasp of its thinking and recommendations. It is not a mere contents list, nor is it an abstract. The target market for the plan's acceptance must be the focus for the executive summary: this audience must be engaged immediately, impressed by the clarity of the proposals and persuaded to consider the recommendations.

The executive summary should briefly state the current situation; this should describe the place of the library or information centre within the overall organization. It should identify trends which will affect the organization and therefore the library or information service, as well as those that will have direct impact on the service. This is evidence of the presenter's knowledge and realistic appraisal and, therefore, the likely sense of their proposals. The summary must state the aims of the plan positively. This is not the place for library history, grand rhetoric or pious hopes. It is introducing, in essence, a business plan, which will use a substantial part of the organization's resources in its implementation. The summary needs to impress upon its audience that, based on sound information and well-thought-through decisions, the plan presented will have a good chance of enhancing the efficiency and strengths of the organization. The key issues are needed, not a long preamble.

The mission statement

Only the relevant elements of the mission statement of the organization need to be repeated here. If there are international, national, regional and local issues for the organization, but the information service supports only the local dimension, then focus on that element. Should the organization be concerned with all aspects of community life but the information centre is concerned with health only, then emphasize that special concern.

The mission of the library or information centre does need to be expressed clearly here, since all that follows stems from that generating force.

The environmental analysis

The monitoring of PEST variables (see page 29–38) should be a continual and essential part of the marketing information system. Here in the marketing plan, the influences from political, economic, social, technological and legal spheres do not need lengthy explanation or analysis. Rather, what needs to be presented is the trend evidence that has led to the strategic decisions. It has been argued that librarians are not risk takers, that they would prefer not to take decisions, but merely present the evidence. But who knows the service better, who knows their clients best, who is likely to make the best decisions regarding services and clients? There may be a risk in predicting in the areas of uncontrollable variables, but the greater risk is to do nothing and risk extinction.

The SWOT analysis

The SWOT analysis (see pages 38–40) presented in the marketing plan should be a distilled version of the detailed SWOT produced during the preparation of the plan. It should identify the key issues that the marketing plan will address. Since the plan is after all a realistic appraisal of what might be achieved, fundamental strengths and weaknesses must be identified, for example a training deficit that may take six months or three years to remedy.

It may seem odd, in a plan that is aiming at persuading an executive to fund its operation, to admit to weaknesses, but it does show objectivity. Equally, when the weaknesses are matched with plans to remedy or compensate them, management will see the need for resources in these areas, whereas if strengths only are emphasized there is a real danger of resource reduction.

An audit of the competition will have shown clearly the current position of the library: a public library in relation to its community and other outlets for recreation, education and information, or perhaps a university or college library losing out to computing units or rival institutions. However, beware highlighting as a threat the fact that the company could buy in information, rather than using its in-house information centre, to an executive board who might not have thought about this excellent idea previously. The information professional should take steps to ensure that the information or service deficit that might push the company to seek information elsewhere becomes an opportunity for development. Either the centre's ability to offer the service needs to be addressed or the information centre should make itself responsible for obtaining what is necessary from the external source, thereby retaining control of its position as sole information provider.

The portfolio analysis

It does make a great deal of sense to treat the various parts of the library or information centre's services as separate entities. The services may be aimed at various markets or have reached different phases of the product lifecycle. There may be acute competition for some markets, whereas in others the library may be the sole provider, but nevertheless operating at a loss.

It may be that a service could well be made available to other market segments, thus developing new markets. Do funds exist to support such developments and has the service the capacity to enter new markets successfully? Would this be a short-term or long-term objective?

The use of the Boston Consulting Group model and Ansoff's matrix (see Chapter 3) will have identified potential areas for development. The marketing plan needs to address these and state why such development might or might not be feasible. It is useful to say briefly why a potential solution has been rejected since it precludes any discussions in the vein of why was such and such not considered? The plan thus demonstrates that alternative solutions exist, while the preferred option is strengthened by the reasoned succinct argument and all the decision makers' energies are focused on the recommendations.

Specific objectives

What, to whom, how, when, and where? Clearly formulated and stated objectives answer these questions. If customer satisfaction is the main aim, and you can't please all of the people all of the time, what is a realistic objective?

Service provision is, on the whole, intangible in nature; it is argued that quality has yet to be defined other than in terms of reliability, but an essential objective common to all library and information services must be to deliver what is promised.

The mission statement encompasses general aims, but the objectives framed in this section must be objective and quantifiable: 'increase market share' should be 'increase market share by 5%'; 'online provision to improve' should be 'increase the rate of provision for undergraduate students within nine months by 50%'; 'support IT skills in the community' should be 'double access to IT facilities within 12 months by training x number of staff to support'.

Market penetration or development can be exemplified and quantified; satisfaction rates or changes in image perception are not so easily ascertained and objectives should be framed bearing this in mind. Objectives and targets will need to be formulated with an awareness of how information or evidence might be collected to show whether or not they have been achieved. Rates of use and numbers of new users can be measured easily. Changes in perception or satisfaction rates can be monitored too, but planning needs to start early and resources to be allocated accordingly for market research.

Objectives must be achievable. The Citizen's Charter in the UK emphasizes specific objectives for services, so that there is hardly an organization remaining in the UK that does not answer letters within 15 days or answer a telephone before the fifth ring. The library that relies on a recorded message for that answer and leaves a user in a queue for an unacceptable time is risking substantial damage to its image as an efficient information provider.

Customer care objectives might depend on building up a committed workforce, which would necessarily demand specifying levels of training and achievement for all staff. Users are aware of 'psychological bowing', employees trained to produce a pat response. This is not the aim. Staff who feel good about themselves and their job will interact more effectively with the user.

User perception and satisfaction testing is an inherent corollary of objectives. This should be stated explicitly, not just for the sake of completeness, but because objectives relate directly to budget needs and resource allocation.

Market segmentation

The marketing plan is an operational plan. Decision makers who are not so familiar with the library or information service may need to be introduced to its value in its particular community and to its broad user-segment categories. The segments to be targeted should then be described and justified.

Some statistics will be more tellingly presented in graphic form. Enlisting the aid of colleagues in other departments to produce them in this format, should the necessary expertise not reside among library staff specialisms, will create interest and enhance valuable linkages.

The proposed groups to be targeted may be the most controversial area of the plan; a university library putting priority on undergraduate provision, or a public library on provision for the business community, will engender heated debate, even if the recommendations are well justified.

Marketing strategies

Justification is vital here. Major resource implications are found in objectives, but it is here that the questions will be asked: is it necessary, will it work, what are the tangible benefits?

Opposition is most likely to be raised when a service is comparatively strong: should resources required for marketing not be used elsewhere in the library or information centre, for new staff, new technology, new sources? The plan should pre-empt this and show that if the recommendations are not acted upon then there is a danger that the service will not develop, but will in all probability weaken. It should also warn that any tendency to complacency needs to be guarded against. To be convincing, strategies and targets need to be set out clearly as the foundation of the action plan.

Market research strategies

Marketing research will have been carried out in the preparation of the plan. The market research that will be necessary as part of the action plan (see Chapter 8) needs to be described in this section. It is necessary to decide at this stage what proportion of the work can be done in-house, and what proportion supplied by an external agent. A timescale should also be included in the plan. The reasons for the research must be set out, together with the data, responses and results sought, and it should be emphasized that it will all help promote more effective use of the required resources.

Marketing mixes recommended

Plans within the plan are required here if more than one service area is being tackled. A whole library or information centre approach in terms of corporate image will have particular objectives that will obviously affect specific services, too, but it is not advisable to aim at one catch-all mix. The researcher in the company's research and development division would be using the same information service as the finance chief or the production manager, but sources, approaches, staff specialisms, access needs and communication modes will all be different and different mixes should be planned. The undergraduate engineer is very different from the member of academic staff in fine arts, and the local businessman has different needs from the pre-schooler's father, even though, in truth, they may be the same person.

Evaluation methods

Evaluation should not be treated as a snapshot for preservation: too many evaluation studies and reports are produced as if they are the final flourish to a programme or an activity before burial in the archives of the organization. Evaluation must be well planned, carried out as an on-going and integrative activity, and the findings used as a tool for improving effectiveness.

Evaluation methods are tied in with a need for market research. Are the objectives being reached, is the plan being implemented fully, have external factors caused it to be amended, how effective has it been? How do you intend to check?

It is important to ensure that evaluation is built into the structure of the plan's proposed implementation. Evaluation should be formative as well as summative and the plan should be flexible enough to accommodate change, if needed, at evaluation stages. The pattern of evaluation proposed needs to be accompanied by an indication of reporting procedures and consequent actions, i.e. who is to receive the information and what decision making is needed as a consequence. Methods of feedback need to be described in the plan.

The timetable

Critical path analysis, project management software packages, knowledge and experience of the library or information centre's environment and users, all will aid in the construction of a relevant and reasonable timetable. 'Just in time' practices could be studied too; for example, a survey questionnaire to a student body needs to be printed early enough so that it can be administered to the undergraduate population well before hectic examination preparation. Plenty of time needs to be allotted for checking legislation; translation into numerous languages can be uneven. Consultation will highlight other potential hazards or hold-ups.

Another aspect of timetabling is to continually check that there is no clash with another activity at crucial points of the plan, whether in the planning stages, implementation or promotion. Peak periods for financial planning, printing, staff holidays, national or religious festivals, can all affect the best-laid plans.

The budget

Financial planning calls for specialist expertise; it is not simply a matter of attaching costs and forecasts to specific budget heads and, again, it is valuable to enlist the help of specialist colleagues.

A check-through of every section of the marketing plan, asking what it entails, who would be involved, what has to happen before this is tackled, is advisable. This will highlight resource and finance implications that may not be immediately obvious: where perhaps the plan producer may believe something is implicit, but this is not apparent to the funding decision makers and needs further explanation. Overheads may well be covered by a parent organization, but double-checking on this is advised. In this area insurance costs, for example, are often overlooked.

Finally

A check of why, what, when, where and, most important, who will result in a convincing and effective marketing plan to take the library and information centre forward into a successful future.

References and further reading

Ace, C. (2001) *Effective promotional planning for e-business*, Butterworth-Heinemann/Chartered Institute of Marketing.

Buzan, T., Dottino, T. and Israel, R. (1999) *The BrainSmart Leader*, Ashgate.

Cohen, W. A. (2001) *The marketing plan*, 3rd edn, John Wiley and Sons.

Cooper, J. and Lane, P. (1997) *Practical marketing planning*, Macmillan.

Corrall, S. (2000) *Strategic management of information services: a planning handbook*, Aslib/Information Management International.

Coulter, M. (2002) *Strategic management in action*, 2nd edn, Prentice Hall.

Etzel, B. (1996) *Personal information management*, Macmillan.

Janal, D. S. (2000) *Dan Janal's guide to marketing on the internet*, John Wiley.

McDonald, M. and Payne, A. (1998) *Marketing planning for services*, Butterworth-Heinemann on behalf of The Chartered Institute of Marketing.

McDonald, M. H. B. (1999) *Marketing plans: how to prepare them, how to use them*, 4th edn, Butterworth-Heinemann.

Rowley, J. (2001) *Information marketing*, Ashgate.

Schulz, E. (2000) *The marketing game*, Kogan Page.

INDEX